BUSINESS DECISIONS

by

Christer Ekman

Klas Mellander

Marie Owens

© Copyright: 1991 Klas Mellander AB
Distribution: Celemiab International AB
ISBN 91-970433-4-6

The Decision Base simulation model was developed over ten years ago, and today it is used the world over. Regardless of culture, economic policy or language, Decision Base is an excellent method for conveying true understanding of business finance and economics. As a result of suggestions from Decision Base seminar leaders, material of a more detailed nature, that the participants can take with them at the conclusion of the Decision Base seminar, has been developed.

About the book

This book has been written primarily for participants in Decision Base seminars. Its purpose is to help them turn their experiences into knowledge. We have tried to cover the material from the most important perspectives, but we encourage the reader to study only the sections that are relevant to his or her particular situation. The introductory chapter asks the question "What does finance have to do with business?" We ask this question because in many companies there is still a tendency to consider finance as a dull exercise in figure juggling, when it should really be seen as a generator of decision making data that will lead to better business.

Part 1 - Making business decisions

So the subject here is decision making. The question we try to answer is "What data and what information are needed to make specific decisions?"

For each main area (department) we describe:

- Critical incidents, i.e. unexpected events that can occur in the life of the department manager.
- The manager's responsibilities.
- "Decision Base illustrations", i.e. examples of how different situations are presented in the simulation.
- Conflicts of interest.

We present these descriptions through the eyes of the corresponding department manager, but they are just as interesting for those working in other departments as they are for those in the department involved. In most companies, inter-departmental communications and understanding are considered the key to total efficiency.

Part 2 - Financial control of the company and its operations

The objective of this publication is not to enable the reader to write an annual report or to develop a strategic plan. Rather, the idea is to cover briefly a wide range of issues and to encourage debate.

Nevertheless, many issues have had to be omitted. Here, the focus is on control and planning. The leadership functions of management and organization are mentioned only in passing. Some control and planning topics have also been skipped, due to space limitations.

Part 3 - Planning

Issues related to control and various planning topics are covered in part three.

Throughout the text, points are illustrated with examples from Decision Base companies' experiences and part three ends with two case studies involving Beta company.

CONTENTS

INTRO-
DUCTION.

INTRODUCTION
What does finance have to do with business?

Most of us intuitively know what "good economy" is. We also have a passable understanding of what "poor economy" is. But what is "economy?" The dictionary says it's "the thrifty use and management of limited resources" - and perhaps that's a good place to start.

The problem with terms like "business administration" and "finance" is that they mean different things to different people. Suppose that the members of a company's management feel that their people in general "have too little financial know-how." (Management people have been known to come to this conclusion!) But what does it mean?

A company's business can be viewed as a circulation of capital.

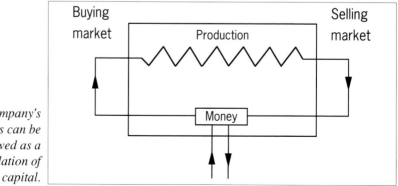

- Does it mean that they are not thrifty enough?
- Does it mean that they can't read a balance sheet and analyze the profitability of the business?
- Does it mean that they know too little about financing and financial cost?
- Does it mean that they can't calculate investments, or don't know how to apply the annuity method or the net present-value method?
- Does it mean that they aren't sufficiently aware of the economic consequences of their actions and can't calculate costs?
- Does it mean that they don't know how to debit a credit account?
- Or does it simply mean that they don't know how to fill in report forms properly?

Obviously the problem of "having too little financial know-how" has several dimensions. Of course we can study business administration and learn for example that costs, expenses and payments are not the same thing - i.e. that very similar concepts have different and specific meanings. Or that the contents of financial statements are translations into monetary terms of items whose value is circumstantial - that is, they can only be literally true with reference to prevailing circumstances. Or that full costing is better than variable costing or vice versa; it can be a matter of opinion or circumstances or even debate which method should be applied in a certain situation.

Could it be that this was far from what the management people mentioned above had in mind when they said that their people "have too little financial know-how?" Perhaps what they really meant is that the personnel's "business sense" - their ability to make day-to-day decisions at all levels on large and small matters - leaves something to be desired, and that they should be more business-oriented.

If so, company financial training programs should focus less on the methods and terminology of economists, and more on how best to use financial data as a basis for decision making. The difference between the two approaches is enormous.

It might be a good idea to start off by presenting the lowest common denominator for the disciplines of "finance" and "business."

It consists of a model showing how capital circulates in a company. Money is spent to purchase materials and other necessary items - materials are delivered to production - materials and man-hours are transformed into products - the products are sold to customers and become accounts receivable - the debt is paid by the customer and again becomes cash.

Our goal in this process is to take in more money than we pay out.

Up to this point, business economics is easy to understand, but when we ask the question "How do we do this?" it gets more complicated.

Understanding the step-by-step transformation of capital into subsequent forms is important. Understanding how this transformation is influenced by the types of investments we make is equally important. Look at Decision Base. It is identical to this model of circulating capital and it provides insight into financial and business economy.

More and more people involved

The idea of greater decentralization is being widely discussed these days. In many places, companies are attempting to organize their people into fairly small and limited "business centers" with sharply defined responsibility for their own finances (their own business). Some companies are pursuing this objective more credibly than others, but in companies where the management has demonstrated through its actions that it means business, measures will have to be taken to ensure that the people involved can act in the ways management had in mind.

Of these measures, training in the traditional sense will probably not be a high-priority item. This opinion is based on the belief that a poor information system isn't likely to get better just because courses are offered about it.

Most financial systems are created by finance people for financial people. These experts give their systems the characteristics they consider important, but as a rule they fail to bridge the gap between their own perspective and that of the people who are going to use the resulting information in their daily work.

People entrusted with responsibility must be provided with information that serves as a guide for everyday decisions - information that tells them what they're doing right and what they're doing wrong.

Few financial information systems today appear to meet this requirement. The following example will illustrate what we mean.

Exercise

A company has an ordinary lathe and a numerical control (NC) lathe. The internal price lists (preparation data) indicate that the cost of operation P depends on which lathe is used: USD 36 with the ordinary lathe and USD 27 with the NC lathe. One day the foreman appears with order X in his hand. According to the planning data (order card), the NC lathe is to be used for the order. But several other jobs that cannot be postponed are waiting in line for this lathe. The ordinary lathe is free at the time.

The person assigning the job (order) has two alternatives:

Alternative 1: He gives order X to the operator of the ordinary lathe. As a result, a large part of the expected profit on

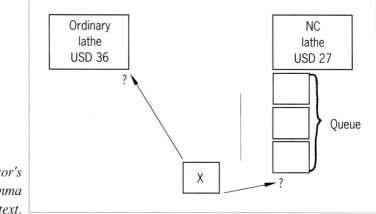

The supervisor's dilemma
See the text.

the order will disappear.

Alternative 2: He gives the order to the operator of the NC lathe as planned. As a result the product won't be delivered on time.

Which alternative should he choose?

Think about it carefully. This question is more important than it appears at first glance.

If these prices had not been established for the operation, the decision would have been easy: He would have assigned the job to the free machine. What makes him think twice is the fact that the operation will be "more expensive." But will it? On paper, perhaps, but not in actual fact.

The example shows that the decision facing the supervisor depends on how the cost of the operation is defined. Most companies can tolerate decisions based on fuzzy perception occasionally, but not if they become the general rule.

P.S. A supervisor commented on the example like this: "If I had been the supervisor in the example, I probably would have assigned the job to the ordinary lathe, but reported that it was run on the NC lathe as planned..."

Obstacles to dialog

All financial reports are subjective. The stringency, logic and mathematics applied in financial statements give the user information that is clear-cut and misleading at the same time.

No one would deny that financial information and financial statements provide only a limited view of the reality they're supposed to reflect. In spite of this, the control instruments a company uses are often based excessively on information obtained from financial information systems. (This is sometimes due to the fact that no other sources are available.)

In every company, people should strive to develop information systems - and thus data for decision making - that provide the information needed to achieve the company's overall goals and to deal with short-term priorities.

We mustn't forget that internal financial reports constitute one of our most important reward systems:

- "You're doing a good job if you achieve higher profits than those stipulated in the budget."
- "You're doing a good job if you keep costs down."
- "You're doing a good job if you can increase sales without increasing sales costs proportionally."

Of couse, these value judgements provide enormous benefits by stimulating the people involved, and by giving them a chance to see how well they have succeeded in achieving the various individual goals.

The problem is that such value judgements also produce a number of other effects which can cause the company to miss important business opportunities.

An information system can be developed only if a dialog is established between decision makers and finance people.

The people in the finance department are asked to provide data for decision making, but this is obviously impossible if they aren't told the nature of the decisions in question.

The way it is now, priority is given to the interpretations of the finance people, so they have much more influence over decisions than they themselves and others really want them to have.

When the decisions are of a more important and sweeping nature, the company is usually capable of compensating for any bias in the decision making data. But other types of bias are more dangerous: Those that insidiously and systematically creep into and become part of the company's system of norms.

For example, study the five illustrations presented on the following pages. They show how differently various companies can view the same phenomenon. Think about this: How do such problems manifest themselves in your company?

That's what they say, but what do they mean?

Using a pencil, paper and clever formulas, one can convince people that an investment is worthwhile. Someone has said that any technician who can't "prove" that his proposed investment is worthwhile is a poor technician.

This is obviously a worthwhile investment...

The problem is that little is actually known about the consequences of an investment. For example, there may be expectations of a certain sales increase, so the proposal is presented together with a calculation which shows that the investment is worthwhile in this regard.

If the proposal is rejected because the predicted sales increase is too optimistic, the company may miss out on other benefits that aren't as easy to calculate: Greater reliability, higher quality, lower levels of tied-up capital, a better working environment, etc. If, on the other hand, the company makes the investment, it will have difficulty determining later how valuable the investment actually was.

The department's
financial results are
unsatisfactory...

Anyone who says this probably means that the department's costs are too high. This can lead to a cost-cutting drive that obliges the department to refrain from doing something that may have been important in the long term. Such action may enable the department to meet this year's budget, but what happens then?

If all of us
sticks to our own job
and do the best we can within
our own area, the company
will be successful...

The truth of this statement is highly uncertain. It's not enough for each member of the company to be an expert in "her own area" and to do her job without considering her function as part of the whole.

The Purchasing Department finished the year way under budget, even though it purchased the budgeted quantities...

That's great... or is it? Suppose the Purchasing Department achieved this by switching suppliers. And suppose that this resulted in delivery delays (and thus production delays). Suppose that the material purchased is of lower quality than the material used earlier. We can celebrate only when we have the answers to such questions.

The department must economize...

Anyone who says this probably means that the department's operations cost more than expected. Perhaps there was a lot of overtime work. Maybe it was necessary to call in outside help because there was an unusual amount of work to do or because there were difficult problems to deal with.

This statement means nothing unless we know what the effects of the cost overrun were. Perhaps the people in the department succeeded in solving certain problems, thereby benefiting considerably another department in the company.

These impressions are meant to give a rough idea of what business administration is and what decision making is all about. The book you are reading will familiarize you with Decision Base, and with how it can teach you to make good strategic and operative business decisions.

PART 1.

Making business decisions

1. The role of the management team - the roles of the managers

The management team

A management team is a very powerful resource. Its members combine their various experiences and their specialized knowledge in their respective fields, i.e. they contribute different pieces of the puzzle, to reach a consensus on ways to develop the company's business and resources, and thus ensure success.

With regard to the company's future, the consensus will cover four basic points:

- A general idea about strategic aims, i.e. what the company will become in the long term.
- How to create a unique market position for the company - how to "expand the market to our advantage," create market niches, etc., instead of just chasing market share.
- An orientation towards target groups in the market or specific market areas that the company will concentrate on.
- A competitive strategy - how to increase relative strength or avoid head-on competition.

Perhaps the most fascinating side of business decision making is its intuitiveness. You combine many factors - some of them based on factual information, some just hunches and feelings, some very temporary and that create opportunities you can take advantage of if you think it's the right thing to do and you dare to do it. You can take such chances if you've managed to get your company into good shape.

How do you do this? How do you prepare for unknown events? That is the management team's challenge. Prepare for something! Decide what you think the future will offer and require, and what the competition will allow you to do. Try to build competitive edge so that some customers will perceive you as the best alternative. Be the leader *somewhere*. Don't just tag along.

There is however a base of sound "mathematics" for business, the "decision base," that lets you control events. Once you master this, you can really start doing some serious decision making.

The department manager

A company's strength is made up of the interacting strengths of the various departments. The effects of an overall strategy on a certain department, be it marketing, production, product development or financing, have to be interpreted and turned into actions by the corresponding manager.

The most important factors, i.e. the "independent variables," are the choices of market investments, product development, marketing policies and production resources. They reflect ambitions to develop positions in various markets, expected trends in product demand and price levels and ideas for creating competitive advantages. Based on this, the team tries to run the company efficiently in terms of resource utilization and economy, and to make sure that the company never runs out of cash. Each manager's decisions and actions have to help the team to achieve these goals.

Let's see what this means. We can describe the roles of the department managers by considering:

- what their responsibilities are.

- what they monitor and control.

- what types of decisions they have to make.

- what information they need for decision making.

but also:

- what critical incidents can affect their departments.

- what conflicts of interest may arise with colleagues on the management team.

- what signals the managers look for as indications of a need for change in their departments.

The understanding of this and the tools that aid in the manager's planning is what we call "decision support". In the following sections we will illustrate this in more detail, keeping in mind the Decision Base simulation.

2. The marketing manager

Critical incidents:

Murphy's law ("If something can go wrong it will") is an important factor in management; bad luck is another. The combination of the two can be rather frustrating and the marketing manager will have his hands full when dealing with some of the situations that come up. Let's look at some things that are likely to happen, one by one. In Decision Base, as in real life, they cause enormous problems.

"An important order cannot be delivered on time because there were delays in production."
Often enough there can be a penalty clause in the contract, so the cost is some money and a loss in market confidence.

> DECISION BASE ILLUSTRATION: Orders cannot be "partially delivered." An order you accept has to be delivered within the year or, if it is an "urgent order," within the first quarter. If you don't, you will have to deliver it before you do anything else during the next period, and you have to pay a penalty equal to 25% of the order value. If you were the market leader, you would lose that position. Causes behind production delays are discussed in the "production manager" section.

"Market price levels turned out to be worse than we had anticipated in our budget."
This will occur late in a product's market life cycle. Perhaps prices would be better in another market than the one we are in now. Such problems can also appear at an early stage: customers are reluctant to change, they may not be prepared to take

full advantage of a new alternative or they may require a lot of extra service.

DECISION BASE ILLUSTRATION: At the market table it may happen for example that Master prices drop to something like 3.3 M per series on the present market. While not directly unprofitable, this level does little to help you cover your overhead. Because order cards are presented for one market area at a time, you may not know whether to accept an order now or wait for the next market area - or keep your production in stock until next year. What you do know is that a year with too few orders and too little volume will put you under a lot of pressure and leave you with a weak market position.

"The customer enquiries presented are bigger than we dare to accept, considering our capacity."
This often happens to small companies. They would prefer to specialize in market niches or at least to have small customers in the general market.

DECISION BASE ILLUSTRATION: The order cards shown are too large for your remaining capacity when it is your turn at the market table. You know what the cost will be for non-delivery, and if you take an order in spite of this, you'll have to rely on cooperating with somebody else.

"We wanted to be the leaders in the .... market, but another company beat us to it by investing more in marketing."
This can be the result of unimaginative market strategy or careless analysis of the competitive situation. "We didn't have the competitive edge we thought we had," or "the marketing campaign we launched wasn't decisive enough."

DECISION BASE ILLUSTRATION: Of course all of the teams hide their market boards in order to guard against industrial espionage. Do you? If you have the same market strategy as some of the other teams, it's going to cost you a great deal to become leader if you rely on brute-force marketing power alone. Just imagine the contribution margin this brawn-instead-of-brains strategy would require. In any case, it is worth making an effort to become market leader, both in Decision Base and in real life.

"Our forecast of market demand turned out to be wrong. Our budget is based on the forecast and, unfortunately, Production and Finance based their plans on our budget." This is all too common. Did we base our forecast on our own volume needs, or on an excessively optimistic estimate of market response?

DECISION BASE ILLUSTRATION: Data for drawing up a forecast can be found most readily in the Market Journal,which is a fairly good information source but not infallible. A market responds with enquiries (order cards) to the marketing efforts of the suppliers. Greater efforts bring out more customers - up to a certain point where the demand levels off, so the market is in your own hands to a certain extent. If the orders being presented don't match your production capacity, either your marketing efforts are too weak or you're out of your league.

"Our main product is approaching the end of its life cycle, and we still don't have a suitable successor ready to take over." Maybe our previous strategy was just a little too successful and in fact prevented us from seeing the "writing on the wall." Innovation is the ally of the attacker and the enemy of the defender. Even if we set out to cannibalize our old standbys, the internal decision making process is full of serious reservations, and judging the best time for a changeover is extremely difficult.

DECISION BASE ILLUSTRATION: The price level given on the order cards provides an early warning. The number of order cards for a specific product in a specific market gives us a later warning. Product development takes at least one and a half years, and it takes a year to complete a production line. In addition, if you continue with a product too long, others may come out with new and better products before you do. If you choose that strategy, you may wind up having to take one giant development step instead of several smaller ones.

"Every business deal is profitable, but we can't get enough volume to cover our overhead."

This may not occur all of a sudden, but it is common in mature industries where competition is heavy. Deals are closed on a short-sighted basis, utilization of existing capacity is more important than price level and, as a result, the total contribution is insufficient.

DECISION BASE ILLUSTRATION: If your company's production facilities lack the necessary efficiency, you'll discover that your indirect costs are getting out of control. On the other hand, if you've built up strong production resources but your competitors have done likewise for the same product, the overall supply may be far above market demand, no matter how much you spend on marketing. Consequently:

"The competitors seem to follow precisely the same strategy as we do, so we are always fighting for the same customers."

Competitive advantages are normally smaller and more difficult to achieve in reality than in strategic plans, although a highly decisive production strategy can sometimes result in real cost benefits, while strong specialization can lead to positioning benefits. We have to differentiate in order to create a market position of our own, but achieving differentiation in an open market situation isn't so easy. The best differentiation is good customer relations: Being first to market is one way; innovation is another. Market leadership is usually relatively easy to hold on to once you've acquired it.

DECISION BASE ILLUSTRATION: Choosing an opening strategy is important in Decision Base. If you invest in the same resources, products and markets as everybody else, your hands will be tied at the market table. Even not investing in anything might give you an advantage, but it will be a short-lived one. If you try to cover too many strategic routes, you'll see the results in your financial reports after a couple of years. Decision Base tends to reward differentiation, market leadership and sound production capacity. If you're first to market you'll be the market leader and, as in real life, being the leader gives you a better chance of remaining the leader.

The marketing manager's direct responsibilities:

Long-term:

- To propose a market strategy for discussion by the team: Market entry - where and when?
- Telling the production manager what production capacity must be developed to cope with market growth:
- Marketing policies and promotion budgets.
- Telling the finance manager how much money will be needed for market investments and marketing.
- Finding out what the competitor's strategies are.

Short-term:

- Obtaining information on market trends and on what the competitors are doing.

- Planning what orders to accept, taking into account product development and production capacity.
- Reporting to the management team on price and demand trends for the various products in the various markets.
- Sales budget for the coming year.

Operational:

- Competing for orders in the market, and winning orders that are profitable for the company.
- Setting delivery priorities in order to achieve optimum economy.

Matters for the marketing manager to monitor and control:

- Matching production resources to market growth.
- The progress and timing of market investments and product development.
- The relation between supply and demand in the market.
- The progress of deliveries, from production to customer.
- Lines of credit to customers.

Decisions that the marketing manager has to make:

Some decisions can be discussed with the team:

- Where and how to achieve market leadership.
- How to react to competitors' moves.

The strategic plans will determine others:

- When to start investing in a new market.
- Whether to remain in a market.
- How much to invest in marketing activities - for what products and in which markets.

Some decisions the marketing manager will have to make on the spot at the market:

- What orders to accept in which markets.
- Whether to sell the entire production capacity or leave finished products in stock for the following year.

Information the marketing manager needs for decision making:

Some of the information is of a strategic nature:

- Market growth forecasts on demand and price levels for the various markets and products.
- Who our real competitors are.
- What resources do our competitors have?

Some of the information is of a more budgetary nature:

- What our production and delivery capacities are for the coming year.
- What the product cost is of the various products.

The marketing manager's conflicts of interest:

Of course, the traditional conflict is between production and marketing. A line results in a relatively inflexible production, but it also provides high output. The line makes it difficult to modify production plans and to switch products, which may be just what the company's marketing needs. On the other hand, a highly flexible type of production facility may be far too slow to be accepted by marketing people. So instead of true flexibility, a balanced mix of relatively specialized facilities may have to be employed.

Can there be conflicts between marketing and finance?

- Cash expenditures for marketing to create a strong position can be a point of contention.

- Credit terms granted to customers can cause short-term financial problems.

- When price levels are low, questions about the marketing manager's foresight can arise.

Signals that indicate that changes are necessary:

As mentioned earlier, price levels and volumes at the market are important signals - early warnings that a life cycle is drawing to a close. The number of orders for a specific product in a specific market may be a later warning. The amount of marketing expenditure necessary to achieve a strong market position may indicate that our competitive strategy is not aggressive enough. Cooperation between other companies may be a forewarning of a change in the industry's structure. You may have to do something similar. The production systems developed by competitors may indicate their market ambitions.

3. The production manager

Production is the area that ties up the company's capital. Of course, this is a consequence of the product development program, but it is the fixed assets - the production equipment - that really bind capital. Capital is tied up in the material flow, which, in many companies, is the largest capital item. The type of production system determines the material flow, and, to a large extent, what the company can economically market and sell, so good interaction between market strategy and production development is something to strive for.

Critical incidents:

What unexpected events can occur in the life of a production manager?

Let's look at a day that started just like any other day. The production manager had finished his morning rounds in the fairly large "old factory". Some changes in the layout of a couple of production departments had just been introduced to give a long-overdue improvement in productivity. The economic results of these departments had been a headache for a while ("slow and expensive"), but now the modernization program was finally under way. The general manager was also in the production manager's office, and the two were discussing the consequences of last Monday's strategic decisions, when...

"A production line is down because of a type 1 timing error - we miscalculated and didn't reorder material in time."
No material means no production this period and no margins, because we had sold our entire capacity for the year. Some customer is bound to be unhappy with our performance and God (speaking through the marketing manager) knows what

that will cost. Can we buy the missing product from another team?

> DECISION BASE ILLUSTRATION: No one wants excess stock, but if you overdo keeping stocks to a minimum and fall into the trap, you'll lose something that cannot be regained.

"Type 2 timing error. Incorrect estimate of time required to modify production system."

Longer than expected: Material is piling up, orders are waiting and it will take longer to put the company's finances on a sound footing. *Shorter than expected:* We're not ready yet; no material has been delivered and expensive equipment must stand idle for a period of time.

> DECISION BASE ILLUSTRATION: In Decision Base this problem is even more apparent than in real life.

"We miscalculated the time needed from product development to creation of production capacity for the new product (type 3 timing error), so we lost valuable time to market."

> DECISION BASE ILLUSTRATION: This kind of timing error isn't so easy to avoid. Decision Base indicates this error very clearly. It will affect you the same way as the previous event.

"Here we have good production capacity, but the marketing people always seem to be interested in orders that are unsuitable for our production program - or they accept too few orders to fill our capacity."

Is this the result of a strategic choice or is it just that the market doesn't want what we are good at making?

> DECISION BASE ILLUSTRATION: Say that you have some well-performing Master lines and the number of orders for Master declines. You also notice that...

"Market prices are dropping too fast!"

DECISION BASE ILLUSTRATION: Maybe we invested heavily in lines for the wrong product. A product's life cycle in a specific market will be indicated very clearly at the market.

The production manager's responsibilities:

Strategic production capacity: Let's start at the market end. The team has determined what products the company should be capable of delivering, and the production manager then has to make sure that the necessary production resources are developed. This often demands heavy investment, so the production manager has to be capable of evaluating investments properly.

Productivity and flexibility: Because market plans are based on assumptions that may prove to be incorrect, it may be necessary to modify the product line to a greater or lesser extent. This means that the production manager has to provide sufficient strategic flexibility in the production system. This often demands a sensitive balance between throughput speed and productivity on the one hand, and flexibility on the other.

New products: When a company opts for a new product, the critical timing between product development and creation of production resources is one of the production manager's responsibilities.

Production planning: On a short-term basis, the marketing manager has to know the company's delivery capacity when competing for orders in the various markets. He or she may have to decide on an order on short notice, so precise production planning, materials planning and capacity utilization are among the production manager's important responsibilities.

Cost and capital: The production manager is responsible for the most costly resources, so he or she also has a great deal of responsibility for the company's finances. Smooth, precise material flows and sound purchasing policies are vital for keeping capital tie-up and costs low.

Thus, the responsibilities of production managers obviously have strategic, tactical and operational aspects.

Matters for the production manager to monitor and control:

- Material flows and the utilization of production capacity are items that the production manager must check on a daily basis.

- In more flexible production systems, the production manager must monitor production planning for the various products, to ensure that it coincides with the flow of incoming orders.

- Since he is responsible for production costs, he should also be aware of prices and margins. Continuing to manufacture and offer for sale a product that is approaching the end of its life cycle in a market can have dire consequences.

Decisions that the production manager has to make:

The production manager's responsibilities include decision making in several specific areas:

- The strategy of a company will normally require the creation of additional capacity, and it will be the task of the production manager to decide which type and level of capacity are most suitable.

- In order to evaluate investments, the production manager must discuss price levels, output volumes, margins and the need for flexibility with the marketing manager.

- He or she will have to discuss financing and economic

limititations with the finance manager.

- From time to time it will be necessary to phase out products and modify the capacity - to introduce new products or to increase productivity.
- Very often the company will sell its entire capacity, down to the very last product unit. The market can punish a company severely for production losses. Timing will then be critical, so the production manager's capacity for logical short-term thinking will be challenged.

Information the production manager needs for decision making:

- The production manager has to know what new products are being developed, early enough to create the necessary production capacity.
- He or she will need some market information - estimated price levels, output volumes and margins - in order to evaluate investments.
- He or she will obviously need market planning information - what the marketing manager wants to market, the volume per product and the required flexibility.

Conflicts of interest:

There is the traditional conflict between marketing and production, described in the "marketing manager" section. The marketing and production managers can each believe sincerely that the other's strategic thinking is inappropriate in the current situation. For the finance manager, heavy investments can be a hot item. If the general manager feels that the production manager is sticking to old favorites ("pet projects") and not observing the market strategy, there will be a conflict.

Signals that indicate
that changes are necessary:

Signs that a product's life cycle is reaching its end: a drop in profit margin, a drop in price levels, and obvious overcapacity in the industry. Signs of an inefficient production system: excessively long lead times and too little capacity to ensure profitable operation, even when utilization is high. Signs of changes in the competitive situation: increases in production capacity by competitors.

4. The finance manager

The finance manager has a double function. One is to ensure that there are sufficient funds to support the established production, product and market development plans, as well as cash for day-to-day operations. The other is to act as company controller, i.e. to understand the financial consequences of the proposals of his or her colleagues, such as profitability, risk exposure and tied-up capital. In addition, he or she must develop a financial strategy for the company, together with the general manager.

Critical incidents for the finance manager:

"We had good control over our financial situation, when the volume of incoming orders suddenly dropped to an excessively low level. Before we had a chance to cut costs, our debt/equity ratio soared over the bank's limit."
Maybe our strategy was a little too expansive and our financial position correspondingly sensitive to variations in operating profits. Maybe we underestimated competitive pressures or overestimated market response. In any case, the drop in volume placed the company in the red temporarily, and this hurt our equity.

> DECISION BASE ILLUSTRATION: The bank is relatively willing to inject capital into a company. The rule of thumb is that the debt/equity ratio should not exceed 4:1. Long-term loans should not amount to more than twice the equity, and the rest should consist of short-term loans with a higher interest rate as a risk premium for the lender. It is quite likely that something like this will happen to your company, and its equity will then shrink for a period of time. If the bank recalls its loans, your problems are certain to increase. In Decision

Base the bank is relatively liberal and is willing to lend you more money to help you survive. The interest on short-term loans is 20%, so you'll have to watch your costs to keep the situation from getting out of hand.

"Whenever we need cash it seems as though we always have to use expensive short-term loans, or even factoring on some occasions, which is really a costly way of raising money. The hardest blow came last month, when we had to sell accounts receivable that were to be paid within the next period, in order to raise money to cover marketing expenses. Talk about a hole in the bucket - 56% annual interest! Certainly no triumph for a finance man. Our credit rating seems to be a big C."

Maybe we're getting what we deserve with regard to loans. Maybe the banks consider our company a risk. Or could it simply be disorder and sloppiness in our financial planning and control? Or that we're not very good at planning ahead? Or that - even though we're not an especially high-risk borrower - we're always giving our financiers very short notice?

DECISION BASE ILLUSTRATION: Long-term loans at favorable interest rates can only be negotiated at the end of each year. If you miss this opportunity, you'll have to rely on your operating income, or on short-term loans which can (only) be negotiated at the beginning of each quarter. If you miss this chance as well, factoring is the only remaining alternative - or selling off assets. Until you manage to develop a substantial business volume, financial costs can well reach a magnitude similar to that of your gross profits if you aren't careful. (The bank should be inflexible on the sequence here. Otherwise, the participants will miss a valuable lesson.)

"Acute shortage of cash!"

What happened? Was it something impossible to foresee? Of course this problem can occur when incoming payments are unexpectedly delayed, when outgoing deliveries are delayed, when timing errors are made in the development of production lines, etc. This can also occur if we're already vulnerable financially and the company's operating income suddenly drops drastically.

> DECISION BASE ILLUSTRATION: You may have many millions in "Accounts receivable," "Stocks of materials," "Materials in production," "Stocks of finished products," etc., but not one penny in "Cash." When this happens, you'll find that you may not be at a point in the checklist where you can negotiate bank loans, so you'll have to do something else. Sell off some assets if you can.

"When bankruptcy threatens"

Payments due. No cash available. No accounts receivable to sell for factoring. No bank willing to extend a line of credit. No assets left to sell off. No other company interested in taking over our resources. All in all, no liquidity... no hope.

> DECISION BASE ILLUSTRATION: Such things do happen. In real life banks are sometimes liberal and sometimes restrictive. The same is true here, but there is normally nothing to be gained by letting a team go out of business, because this would bring the participants' learning experience to an end. Instead the team is allowed to work out some arrangement. The company can negotiate a merger with another company. Combining resources can provide synergy effects in production and marketing that could justify a joint venture. The company can agree to become a subcontractor in order to

survive. Decision Base sets no specific rules for negotiations between companies, as long as you negotiate in accordance with good business practices. In cases where the instructor must act as intermediary, he or she will try to settle things in a way that makes it interesting for everyone involved to continue.

The finance manager's direct responsibilities:

Long-term:

- Estimating capital requirements in accordance with the company's development plans.
- Estimating operating income in accordance with the market plan.
- Proposing profitability and debt/equity ratio targets.
- Developing a modern, flexible bookkeeping system.

Short-term:

- Liquidity planning for the current year.
- Arranging financing by means of long-term and/or short-term loans.
- Maintaining good working relations with banks and other finance institutions.
- Adapting the bookkeeping system to new strategic requirements.

Operational:

- Ensuring that sufficient cash is available for day-to-day payments.
- Cash management, i.e. systems for efficient control of accounts receivable and payable, payment terms on contracts, payment dates, short-term investments of surplus cash, etc.

- Periodic financial reports, i.e. Profit & Loss Statements, Balance Sheets and financial analyses.

Matters for the finance manager to monitor and control:

- Operational profitability, i.e. revenues and cost of incoming orders.
- Payments when orders are delivered
- The cash level and short-term cash requirements
- Accounts receivable and payable
- Payment dates for loans and dates for financial decisions.
- The level of general expenses.

Decisions that the finance manager has to make:

- Financing: What kind of loans to take and when. Renewal of loans that fall due.
- Assets: Whether to buy or rent factories.
- Liquidity: The cash level, the use of factoring, the use of surplus cash.

Information the finance manager needs for decision making:

External information:

A real-life finance manager has to keep track of a lot of external information: the current status of various financing instruments and options, trends in interest rates, trends in payment terms and risk exposure in various markets, currency fluctuations, the growth of global financial information systems, fluctuations in world market price levels for relevant commodities and materials, economic forecasts, advances in the development of technical tools like computerized administrative and communications systems, etc. These things are outside the scope of Decision Base, but Decision Base does include some external information, such as market information and customer enquiries, that indicate demand and price trends. This information is highly relevant for a company controller. Internal information:

The most important information here involves cash requirements for the coming period: marketing budgets, production development, product development, market investments and incoming orders.

The finance manager's conflicts of interest:

Acting as company controller, a finance manager may find reason to question the wisdom of anyone who creates expenditures. The marketing manager may be spending too much on marketing in various markets and then accepting orders the head of finance finds unprofitable. The production manager may have embarked on an investment program that is too costly. Even the general manager can be the subject of criticism for allowing a strategy that is too expansive.

Signals that indicate that changes are necessary:

The finance manager is the sentinel for financial dangers that may lie ahead, while the marketing manager is more of a sentinel for opportunities. A decline in profits is a powerful signal for the finance manager. A decline in price levels and in the demand for a product we want to produce is also a signal that we may have to review our strategy.

5. The general manager

Some people are more concerned with the results and needs of their own department than they are with those of the company as a whole. This phenomenon is called "suboptimizing." The word has a somewhat negative ring, but in industry, suboptimizing is a natural consequence of the departmental organization that a company normally needs. The general manager has to ensure that decision making authority and responsibilities are delegated in a way that leads to favorable effects for the company as a whole, i.e. positive synergies between the various suboptimization forces. This involves leading the strategic process, setting goals, pointing out consequences and maintaining an external information network.

The general manager can think of him or herself as "the first among equals" - a leader by virtue of his or her deeds or disposition. In Decision Base, decision making really is a team effort and not a matter of hierarchical superiority. The role of the general manager can well be an educational one: ensuring that the team members work with each other efficiently, and allowing each member to run his or her department while demanding that a consensus be reached on strategic matters.

Critical incidents:

"Gradually it's becoming clear that our strategy has failed. We obviously don't have the advantages we thought we'd have at the market, and at current prices we'll go under within a couple of years."

How did it happen and what can we do to get out of this situation? Of course we have to reexamine our strategy and look for new ideas. If our products don't meet market demands, our whole business idea has to be questioned. If tough competition is the problem, how can we position our company differently in the market?

DECISION BASE ILLUSTRATION: At the market you may find two things: 1) There are not nearly enough enquiries to absorb available capacity. Unless you can change over to other products, your fixed costs will drag you down. 2) You don't succeed in achieving market leadership or first choice of orders, not even by making temporary, heavy marketing investments. Other companies get the best and the most orders. (That's what's so nice about being market leader: you have first choice of orders in each round, and this stabilizes your utilization of production resources.) Of course you studied the market journal before deciding on a strategy, but did you study your competitors' strategies? In any case, the time it takes to make strategic changes will be painfully costly if such changes aren't made early.

"My team is falling apart. Each of the members seems to have a 'pet project' that he or she is pushing hard, and they aren't working together. The production manager is planning to use resources in a way that obviously doesn't coincide with what the marketing manager is aiming for with his marketing strategy."

If we can decide on one business idea, there is no reason why we shouldn't reach consensus on how we should use our resources. Often though, we think we have reached agreement, but when we get down to brass tacks we discover differences in our viewpoints. For example: If the marketing manager opts for high-quality/high-price specialization, then flexibility and high-quality resources are required in production. But if the production manager chooses high-volume/low-cost resources, he or she will guide investments in the latter direction. We will in fact be pursuing two business ideas simultaneously. Just see what happens when a strategy fails to take into account possible results.

DECISION BASE ILLUSTRATION: Right or wrong, production will win the argument, because you can only sell what you have the capacity to produce within the year. But it takes a year to set up a line and it costs a great deal, so production investments demand long-term market planning.

"Our relatively good financial position suddenly weakens and we have the feeling that it's for keeps."
The financial downturn comes after the strategy fails or the business environment changes. Did we rest on our laurels too long? Did we miss some early warning signs? If so, should we start a quick search for a strategic partner who has what we lack and needs what we have in terms of resources? If we wait it may soon be impossible for us to take any initiatives at all.

DECISION BASE ILLUSTRATION: This can also happen in Decision Base. At the start, your company is independent and competes with the other companies, but after a few years a team may find itself in a situation like this one. You are free to negotiate with other teams in accordance with sound business principles. If you wait too long you are likely to become a victim instead of a victor, just as in real life.

"Somebody else's financial position suddenly weakens drastically."
An opportunity for us! What assets does that company have? What possible synergies with us? Can we merge with it? Is this an opportunity to restructure the industry?

DECISION BASE ILLUSTRATION: Keep your eyes open and brush up on your negotiating and calculating skills. You can do this in Decision Base as well as in real life.

"Severe cash problems"

This is the next step in the sequence after a strategy fails - or maybe it's not as bad as it looks. Check your liquidity planning procedure.

> DECISION BASE ILLUSTRATION: Without relatively good financial planning, this can be the result. (No compromises are allowed on the order of the check lists for each quarter, the end of the year and the start of the coming year.)

The general manager's direct responsibilities:

Strategic:

- Human resources: to develop a good management team, each of whose members has clear-cut individual responsibilities, but who can also work well together.
- Scope of company operations: To guide the company into business areas in which the company can achieve a good position.
- To lead the team's strategic planning: to ensure that consensus is reached on the business idea and strategic aims.

Tactical:

- Cooperation with other companies: offensively, through inter-company trading of finished products or production capacity, and defensively, via negotiations on mergers or joint ventures when the company is in crisis.

Operational:

- To analyze financial indicators, market information and competitors' strategies, and to define the issues currently of greatest importance for the company's progress.
- To maintain lines of communication within the company.
- To settle conflicts.

Matters for the general manager to monitor and control:

- Teamwork - must be harmonious and efficient.
- The product/market mix, product development and the development of production capacity.
- Trends in profitability, prices and market demand
- Financial indicators
- (In Decision Base the general manager should call for execution of the procedure as indicated in the check lists for each quarter, etc.)

Decisions that the general manager has to make:

- Hire and fire managers, reorganize the team, etc.
- External cooperation, strategic alliances, product exchanges with other companies.
- How the company's decision making processes should be set up.
- The general manager must have the last word on strategic matters.

Information needed for decision making:

- The company's financial growth.
- The condition of the industry as a whole, what competitors are doing and planning, etc.
- A feeling for the life cycles of products and markets.
- The experiences of his or her department managers.

Conflicts of interest:

This depends. Normally, general managers should be able to stay above any conflicts of interest within the company, but they can have conflicts of their own. This occurs when there is a difference between what the owners want and what the general manager feels is right for the customers in the market. This can result in a situation in which the general manager believes that following the owners' instructions is actually against their own interests. Managers of local subsidiaries of international companies often find themselves in this predicament. This can also occur when a company has to merge with or sell out to another company following a crisis.

Signals that indicate that changes are necessary:

The general manager should get such signals from the other team members. If not, he or she had better watch out.

PART 2.

Financial control of the company and its operations

Introduction

In economic theory a firm is defined as an entity that makes decisions with respect to the production and sale of commodities and services.

The firm is in business to make profits, and thus increase the value of the firm and the earnings of its shareholders. It is well known that some businessmen and businesswomen are inspired by motives other than an overwhelming desire to make as much money as possible. They may seek political influence or have philanthropic motives. It is also possible that managers seek to maximize their own wealth rather than the shareholders'. However, regarding firms as profit maximizing entities is a useful simplification.

Different forms

There are three major forms of business organization: The proprietorship, the partnership, and the corporation. In the proprietorship there is a single owner who is personally responsible for the business. The partnership has two or more joint owners, each of whom is personally responsible for the business. The corporation is regarded in law as a separate entity, and the owners (shareholders) are not personally responsible for the business. The owners elect a board of directors who hire managers to run the firm under the board's supervision. Should the company go bankrupt, the personal liability of any one shareholder is limited to whatever that shareholder has actually invested in the business, which is the money spent to purchase shares. This is called limited liability.

How well the company performs in the marketplace depends on the degree to which the company caters to the market's needs. The ideal firm examines its environment for opportunities, sets appropriate organizational goals, builds a framework for operations, and designs management systems to enable the organization to carry out its strategy.

Planning and control

The following text focuses on planning and control, and on the link between them. Planning is an analytical and decision-making process that ends when a specific plan has been developed. Plans are based on ideas for achieving specific objectives. It is at the action-taking stage that we move into control, which can be defined as the process which attempts to insure that actions conform to plans. We see that control cannot take place without a plan, and a plan cannot be implemented without some control of its progress.

The organization of a firm's operations has to be adapted to the established goals. Different objectives require different kinds of organization. Producing a standardized product requires efficient assembly-line techniques, whereas certain services may require teams of professionals and customized production systems. Goods can be manufactured at long distances from the point of consumption, while services must often be produced at the location where they are to be used. The targeted market share also influences the organization. High-volume businesses require different facilities than a small business.

After plans have been made and the structure of the organization has been determined, the next step is to staff the organization and lead it towards its goals. Leadership is a highly concrete undertaking. It involves working directly with people and getting the members of the organization to perform in ways that will help the company achieve its objectives.

Many businesses start out small, with perhaps a single entrepreneur handling the entire operation. As the business grows and the workload increases, it becomes necessary to group employees into departments. Dividing up the work makes it easier to get things done, and productivity increases. At the same time, it also becomes necessary to coordinate the work of the various departments. Without coordination, departments would begin to pursue their own special interests, often at the expense of the company's overall goals. The interdependence between company departments is one of the major lessons of Decision Base. We will keep that in mind throughout this text.

2.1. Accounting

Accounting is the recording and summarizing of the economic consequences of a company's activities.

The most common way to record a company's transactions is called double-entry bookkeeping. As the name implies, every transaction is recorded twice, once as a debit and once as a credit.

This makes it possible to derive periodic reports (annual, quarterly, monthly), primarily the Profit & Loss Statement and the Balance Sheet.

There are four classes of accounts:

1. Assets

2. Liabilities

3. Revenues

4. Expenses

There are several accounts of each class and the idea is to sort and total the various items systematically. When accounting is done manually every account looks like a "T" with the name of the account on top of the "T". Generally the left side is the Debit side and the right side is the Credit side. You can think of debit as inflow to the account and credit as outflow from it. Accounting can be computerized by giving each account a number which indicates its class and type.

Money flowing into a company will be noted on the debit side of the Cash account and money flowing out will be noted on the credit side of the same account.

To make it easier to understand how a specific transaction is recorded, look at it as inflow to or outflow from **the account itself.**

Example

1. If you buy a piece of material and pay cash for it, record the cost on the debit side of Materials and on the credit side of Cash.

Materials		Cash	
Debit	Credit	Debit	Credit
2 M			2 M

2. If you deliver a product to a customer and send an invoice, record it as an inflow to Accounts receivable and an outflow from Products sold (we call it Sales).

Accounts receivable		Sales	
Debit	Credit	Debit	Credit
10 M			10 M

And so on. Recording transactions in this way can sometimes be difficult, but if you do it right, there will be no ambiguity in your accounts.

The 1986 bookkeeping for a Decision Base company is shown on the following pages. The transaction numbers indicated in the text correspond to the numbers shown in the left-hand portions of the debit and credit sections of the corresponding accounts.

Only the T-accounts needed for the example are included.

1. Enter the opening balance (OB) of the accounts. Note that the OB total for liability accounts is located on the credit side, i.e. on the right-hand side, of each account. (Use the 1985 Balance Sheet.)

Follow the check list for the coming year: (The description below does not cover all of the items in the check list. Only those applicable to 1986 have been included.)

2. **Pay taxes**: Credit account no. 1 (Cash) with 1 M and debit account no. 8 (Short-term liabilities) with the same amount. Since this tax corresponds to last year's profit, it was recorded as a cost last year, affecting account no. 24 (Taxes). This year we merely pay our debt, which affects our cash balance but does not affect this year's costs.

3. **Market and sell**: Credit Cash and debit account no. 12 (Marketing) with 1 M.

Follow the check list for each quarter:

4. **Update the accounts receivable**: Move 6 M from "Accounts receivable" into "Cash," and debit Cash and credit account no. 2 (Accounts receivable) with 6 M.

5. **Take delivery and pay for materials**: Take 2 M from "Cash", put 1 M in each of the two empty cost carriers in "Purchase orders" and move them into "Material and components." Credit Cash and debit account no. 3 (Material and components) with 2 M.

6. **Update the status of ongoing production**: Move all cost carriers in the factory one step to the right (department C empty). Debit account no. 5 (Finished goods) and credit account no. 4 (Work in process, WIP) with 2 M.

7. **Start new production - pay costs**: Move one cost carrier from "Material and components" into "Department C" after paying production costs in advance: Credit Cash with 1 M, credit Material and components with 1 M and debit WIP with 2 M.

8. **Pay quarterly overhead**: Credit Cash and debit account no. 14 (Overhead) with 1 M.

Second quarter:

9. Update the accounts receivable: Debit account no. 1 and credit account no. 2 with 6 M.

10. Take delivery and pay for materials: Credit account no. 1 and debit no. 3 with 2 M.

11. Update the status of ongoing production: Debit account no. 5 and credit no. 4 with 4 M (departments B and D empty).

12. Start new production - pay costs: Credit account no. 1 with 2 M, credit account no. 3 with 2 M and debit account no. 4 with 4 M.

13. Pay quarterly overhead: Credit account no. 1 and debit account no. 14 with 1 M.

Third quarter:

14. Take delivery and pay for materials: Credit account no. 1 and debit no. 3 with 2 M.

15. Update the status of ongoing production: Debit account no. 5 and credit no. 4 with 2 M (department A empty).

16. Start new production - pay costs: Credit account no. 1 with 1 M, credit account no. 3 with 1 M and debit account no. 4 with 2 M.

17. **Deliver finished products and indicate new accounts receivable**: Take 8 cost carriers (each containing 2 M) from "Stock" and trade them in for "Accounts receivable" of 36 M (as agreed on the order card). Credit account no. 5 and debit account no. 21 (Cost of goods sold) with 16 M. Debit account no. 2 with 36 M and credit account no. 20 (Sales) with the same amount.

18. Pay quarterly overhead: Credit account no. 1 and debit account no. 14 with 1 M.

Fourth quarter:

19. Update the accounts receivable: Debit account no. 1 and credit account no. 2 with 36 M.

1. Cash

OB	17	2)	1
4)	6	3)	1
9)	6	5)	2
19)	36	7)	1
		8)	1
		10)	2
		12)	2
		13)	1
		14)	2
		16)	1
		18)	1
		20)	2
		22)	2
		23)	1
		24)	2
		25)	4
		BS	39
	65		65

2. Accounts Receivable

OB	12	4)	6
17)	36	9)	6
		19)	36
	48		48

3. Material & Components

OB	3	7)	1
5)	2	12)	32
10)	2	16)	1
14)	2	22)	2
20)	2	BS	5
	11		11

4. Work in Process

OB	8	6)	2
7)	2	11)	4
12)	4	15)	2
16)	2	21)	4
22)	4	BS	8
	20		20

5. Finished Goods

OB	8	17)	16
6)	2	BS	4
11)	4		
15)	2		
21)	4		
	20		20

6. Real Property

OB	20	BS	20
	20		20

7. Plant & Equipment

OB	8	26)	3
		BS	5
	8		8

8. Short-term Liabilities

2)	1	OB	1
BS	3	27)	3
	4		4

9. Long-term Liabilities

BS	20	OB	20
	20		20

10. Equity

BS	55	OB	55
	55		55

12. Marketing

3)	1	PL	1
	1		1

14. Overhead

8)	1	PL	4
13)	1		
18)	1		
23)	1		
	4		4

15. Department Overhead

25)	4	PL	4
	4		4

16. Rental Costs

	0	0
	0	0

20. Sales

PL	36	17)	36
	36		36

21. Cost of goods sold

17)	16	PL	16
	16		16

22. Depreciation

26)	3	PL	3
	3		3

23. Interest

24)	2	PL	2
	2		2

24. Taxes

27)	3	PL	3
	3		3

PL = Accounts related to the Profit & Loss Statement.
BS = Accounts related to the Balance Sheet.

20. Take delivery and pay for materials: Credit account no. 1 and debit no. 3 with 2 M.

21. Update the status of ongoing production: Debit account no. 5 and credit no. 4 with 4 M (departments C and D empty).

22. Start new production - pay costs: Credit account no. 1 with 2 M, credit account no. 3 with 2 M and debit no. 4 with 4 M.

23. Pay quarterly overhead: Credit account no. 1 and debit account no. 14 with 1 M.

Follow the check list for the end of each year:

24. **Update and pay interest on long-term loans**: Credit account no. 1 and debit no. 23 (Interest) with 2 M.

25. **Pay department overhead**: Credit account no. 1 and debit no. 23 with 4 M (4 x 1).

26. **Indicate depreciation**: 33% of the value of plant and equipment should be credited to account no. 7 (Plant & equipment) and debited to account no. 22 (Depreciation) i.e. 3 M.

Annual reports

Your bookkeeping includes every transaction that has taken place, so you can summarize what has happened to your company's assets and liabilities and you can find out how well your revenues covered your costs. First let's close the books for the year. Accounts 1 to 10 in our example are all in classes 1 and 2, which are to be taken up in the Balance Sheet (BS). Accounts 11 to 25 are related to the Profit & Loss Statement (PL), because they are all in classes 3 and 4. Let's start by preparing the Profit & Loss Statement and then continue with the Balance Sheet.

First, however, each account must itself be balanced, i.e. the difference between the debit and credit totals will be the closing balance for the account. (In our illustration on page 55, we have marked the closing balance for accounts related to the Profit & Loss Statement with PL and for accounts related to the Balance Sheet with BS.)

After listing the closing balance for all accounts in classes 3 and 4 the Profit & Loss Statement will show the result *before* taxes. (To the left on the opposite page.)

27. The tax rate is assumed to be 50%, so half of the indicated profit (the difference between revenues and expenses) is recorded as a short-term liability (credit account no. 8 and debit account no. 24 with 3 M.

Adjust the Profit & Loss Statement accordingly. (To the right on the opposite page.)

Now it's time to balance all of the accounts in classes 1 and 2 and to create the Balance Sheet in the same manner. Then add the profit *after* taxes.

If all of this is done correctly, the Balance Sheet's debit and credit totals will be equal. In addition, double-entry bookkeeping also ensures that the result shown in the Balance Sheet will match that of the Profit & Loss Statement. Thus any transaction that affects the company's profit will in fact be

Profit & Loss Statement
before taxes

Expenses		Revenue	
11. Enter new markets	0	20. Sales	36
12. Marketing	1		
13. R & D	0		
14. Overhead	4		
15. Departm. overhead	4		
17. Product changeovers	0		
18. Factoring fees	0		
19. Miscellaneous	0		
21. Cost of goods sold	16		
22. Depreciation	3		
23. Interest	2		
	30		
Profit	6		
	36		36

Profit & Loss Statement
after taxes

Expenses		Revenue	
11. Enter new markets	0	20. Sales	36
12. Marketing	1		
13. R & D	0		
14. Overhead	4		
15. Departm. overhead	4		
16. Rental Costs	0		
17. Product changeovers	0		
18. Factoring fees	0		
19. Miscellaneous	0		
21. Cost of goods sold	16		
22. Depreciation	3		
23. Interest	2		
24. Taxes	3		
Profit	3		
	36		36

Balance Sheet

Assets		Liabilities & Equity	
1. Cash	39	8. Short-term Liabilities	3
2. Accounts Receivable	0	9. Long-term Liabilities	20
3. Material & Components	5	10. Equity	55
4. Work in Process	8	Profit	3
5. Finished goods	4		
6. Real Property	20		
7. Plant & Equipment	5		
	81		81

recorded once in a Balance Sheet account and once in a Profit & Loss account.

The closing balance shown on the Balance Sheet will then constitute the opening balance for the following year's Balance Sheet. This process will be repeated every year, as long as our company exists.

The Profit &Loss Statement shows the summarized financial result of the company's activities over a one-year period (the accounting period). The Balance Sheet is a summary of the company's financial situation at a specific point in time - i. e. December 31 of the year in question. Study the company's Annual Reports for several different years to get a reliable picture of the situation. Deliveries, prices and costs will vary from year to year. Consider for example that a finished product is recorded as having a book value equal to its material and production cost, but when it is sold it is instantly given a value equal to the sales price. Thus the result figure for the year will depend very much on whether the products were sold or just placed in stocks of finished products, even though the work performed and resources consumed were the same in both cases.

DECISION BASE ILLUSTRATION: In Decision Base, accounting is replaced by the transactions actually taking place, as indicated by the cost carriers on the board. The few notes you

may have to take during the year will involve the revenues and costs that arise when you deliver an order, especially if something extraordinary occurred, such as purchasing from or selling to another team, late delivery, etc. The board will in fact show the Balance Sheet (assets and liabilities) at each instant. It will also show the general expenses that you have incurred. The financial statement that we use summarizes everything that has taken place on the board, and it is highly comparable to that of any real company.

Cash Flow analysis

Cash flow must be analyzed because it provides early signs of changes that will show up later in the Profit & Loss figures. In the Annual Report, cash flow is shown in what is called the Statement of Changes in Financial Position. This statement includes Sources of Funds, Application of Funds and Change in Working Capital. It shows how the company has raised money and to what use it has been put. This Statement is different from the Profit & Loss Statement because in that it shows how the money was spent, rather than the profit or loss.

DECISION BASE ILLUSTRATION: To the right we see a Statement of Changes in Financial Position for a Decision Base company in 1986. In the Statement of Changes in Financial Position, depreciation is added to net income because it reduces profits without affecting our funds. New issues of stock and new loans, if any, would also be added. Changes in other assets would include profits or losses from sales of fixed assets. The total change in sources of funds must equal the total change in the use of funds. In Decision Base 1986 the increase in funds has been used to augment working capital. The money could have been used for investments, loan repayments, or cash dividends.

The change in working capital is shown above, line by line, and is straightforward. Note, however, that increases in liabilities decrease the amount of working capital.

DECISION BASE ILLUSTRATION: As another example suppose that Beta in 1989 had this situation: The stocks of finished goods had increased from two Master series to six. Receivables had decreased from 40 M to 15 M. Short-term loans had increased by 20 M, to a total of 40 M (debt-financed investments). In Cash there was an increase of 5 M. Beta's working capital thus diminished by 32 M. The need to maintain a certain level of working capital became apparent to Beta's managers.

They decided to analyze the situation further. Breaking down the

STATEMENT OF CHANGES IN FINANCIAL POSITION: 1986

Sources of funds

Net income	3
Depreciation (added back)	3
Total from operation	6
Change in equity	0
Loans	0
Changes in other assets	0
Total change, sources of funds	6

Application of funds

Net investments in property, plant and equipment	0
Long-term debt reductions	0
Cash dividends	0
Change in Working Capital	6
Total change, application of funds	6

Change in working capital

Current assets	
Cash	22
Receivables	-12
Inventories	-2
Prepaid expenses	0
Current liabilities	
Notes payable to bank	0
Currently maturiting long-term debt	0
Accounts payable	0
Accrued expenses	0
Accrued income taxes	-2
Change in Working Capital	6

working capital line by line and expressing it as a percentage of Beta's turnover produced the following figures:

Percent of turnover

Cash	10 %
Accounts receivable	25 %
Inventory	20 %
Other current assets	5 %
—	
Total current assets	60 %
Short-term loans	- 30 %
Working capital requirements	30 %

Based on this analysis, Beta's managers concluded that with every 10 M increase in turnover, the need for working capital increases by 3 M.

Analyzing annual reports

The financial statements give you a good idea of the company's performance and situation. For the trained observer studying them is a rather straightforward process. This will be described in more detail later. There can however be complications. Here are some examples: Transactions are reported in accordance with accounting practices and laws, as well as tax regulations. Recently many U.S. companies appeared to have increased their profits. A 15% increase was reported from the first quarter in 1988 to the same period in 1989. Taking a closer look at what this increase consists of, we find that part of it can be explained by the change in the law on depreciation. Accelerated depreciation (depreciation faster than wear and tear) used to be allowed, but no longer. So investment costs have to be spread out over a longer period of time, with a smaller portion of the total each year. This makes it look as though the company has increased its profits. Another factor is rising supplier prices. Higher supplier prices raise the value of existing inventory (valued at replacement cost), so on paper, profits increase.

If the company being studied is a member of a Group, it is a good idea to study the consolidated report for the entire Group. But such information is not always readily available. In Japan consolidated group accounts were not required by law until 1989.

The way in which a company finances itself can also affect the figures. A bank-financed company tries to impress bankers, and bankers look for a stable core business. So the company's goals would be low risk, stable growth and minimum annual taxes. On the other hand, an equity-financed company wishing to attract investors might prefer to show high profitability, market innovation, etc.

Cash flow and liquidity planning

Earnings are recorded in the books when the invoice is sent, not when the customer pays the bill, so it's not always easy to translate accounting data back into actual dollars that you can buy beer with.

Cash flow is a company's source of funds. It is the stream of incoming and outgoing payments that have to balance in the long run. Liquidity planning involves forecasting in detail the payments for the coming period to ensure that there will be enough money on hand to cover operating expenses. If your company is in a tight financial position you will quickly become aware of the importance of liquidity planning and cash flow control. If your business is trading, following the cash flow on a daily basis is the natural way to exercise financial control. In all businesses where the turnover is high in relation to equity, cash flow control is more important than return on capital.

Checking the cash flow on a yearly basis is what we did in the Statement of Changes in Financial Position. Because we started with the bottom line (net income) and worked backwards we had to add back transactions that had affected profits but that were not actual payments. Depreciation was obviously one such transaction.

A firm expecting an increase in sales will have expenses to pay before any cash inflows have been generated, such as wages and investments in machinery. Even when products are sold there will be a time lag before the accounts receivable are converted to cash. In a profitable firm the cash inflows will eventually cover the outflows. However, growing firms often run short on cash. With the help of careful liquidity budgeting, difficult periods can be planned for and the firm can obtain additional cash from banks and other sources. Speeding up the cash flow cycle will also relieve a liquidity squeeze. This can be done by reducing the time from production to sales to collection. Just-in-time stock management and shorter credit terms to customers might prove beneficial. Cash flow is of course sensitive to conditions outside the company as well. Increases in interest rates will hit leveraged companies the hardest, while higher inflation rates will affect all firms.

Let's return to the American companies' rise in profits and see how this relates to cash flow. We've already mentioned the higher value of inventory. Such profits are not included in the cash flow because the inventory has to be restocked at a higher price. The result of slower depreciation is higher reported earnings. But since earnings are taxed and depreciation is not, the effect is a reduction in the company's cash flow. Interestingly enough, the U.S. Department of Commerce reports that if the effect of inventory profits and accounting changes are excluded, companies' after-tax profits actually fell 5% between the first quarter of 1988 and the same period in 1989.

Cash flow is related to capital turnover. The latter indicates how many times you put your dollars to use during a given period. A higher capital turnover rate generates more cash flow - of both income and expenses. Clearly you want to get as much mileage as possible out of your cash. A low capital turnover rate should alert you to identify and eliminate bottlenecks.

Budgeting

The most widely-used tool for planning and controlling activities at all levels of an organization is the budget. Budgets are formal statements of the financial resources set aside for carrying out specific activities in a given period of time. A budget contains estimated figures for expenditures, revenues, and profits. You can thus budget the company's liquidity, capital expenses, personnel, and so on. The total of this is the company's overall budget. The figures contained in the budget are the goals, and the information in the books tells whether you've strayed from the budget.

Strategic planning before budgeting

For the budget to work as desired, the budgeting work must be carried out with great care and intelligence. Simply increasing last year's figures by some random percentage serves no purpose.

The company's overall strategy and goals have to be translated into the numbers that make up the budget. The fundamentals of strategic planning are presented in chapter 3. The Break-Even Analysis described in chapter 2.3 is a simple but valuable tool for monitoring the health of your budget. The item to be analyzed can be a year of production, a product development project, a marketing campaign, a show, a conference, etc. Whenever there is a substantial fixed cost or certain fixed outlays the break-even analysis can help you check and adjust price levels, risk levels, sensitivity to market changes and so on.

The budgeting process is not only a control mechanism, but also an important means of coordinating the company's activities, and of enabling the corporate strategy to filter down to managers and subordinates. In this context the budget can be an important source of motivation. Goals should be difficult but attainable, and the resources set aside to achieve such goals have to be adequate. This will stimulate and challenge employees to improve their performance and meet the budget goals. Employees may not accept goals that are set too high or a tight expense budget, and their performance might actually drop. To this we must add the extra costs of further attempts to coordinate and motivate employees.

THINK ABOUT:

- How employees at your company can become more involved in the budgeting process.

- How results can be communicated when budgets are used to control and motivate employees.

- How external and internal auditing can be used not only to encourage honesty but also to achieve higher operating efficiency.

DECISION BASE ILLUSTRATION: You can run Decision Base without doing much budgeting work – just call the bank when you run out of cash. Thirty years ago most companies didn't have much organized budgeting, but if you want to run your Decision Base company economically and increase your control, the department managers and the general manager should do some formal planning. As an example let's take the Decision Support Notepad for the finance manager. There we can see the liquidity budget for the coming year, which is the finance manager's most important planning tool in Decision Base. (See the next page.)

Finance manager (Fin. mgr.)
DECISION BASE

Year: 1990

Cash flow analysis

Input from	AT THE BEGINNING OF THE YEAR					
Board	Opening cash balance for the year	24				
Balance sheet	1. Pay tax	4				
Mkt. mgr.	3. Enter new markets	1				
Mkt. mgr.	4. Market and sell	12				

	EACH QUARTER	Q1	Q2	Q3	Q4
	Opening cash balance (each quarter)	7	6		
Board	1. Update accounts receivable	24	12		
	Balance + incoming cash	31	18		
	NEEDS/DECISIONS				
	Proceeds from factoring less cost				
	Proceeds from equipment sales				
	Proceeds from property sales				
	2 c. New short-term loans		20		
	Total additional incoming cash		20		
	Total cash	31	38		
	OUTGOING CASH				
Board	2a. Payment of short-term loans				
Board	2b. Interest on short-term loans	2	2		
Team	3. Invest in R&D	4	4		
Prod. mgr.	4. Pay for materials	12	12		
Prod. mgr.	7a. Plant changeover		2		
Team	Purchase of property				
Team	7b. Invest in new equipment	4	4		
Prod. mgr.	8. Start new production, pay costs	2	2		
	10. Pay quarterly overhead	1	1		
	Total outgoing cash	25	27		
	Ending cash balance (each quarter)	6			

AT THE END OF THE YEAR	
Ending cash balance quarter 4	
1a. Payment of long-term loans	
1 b. Interest on long-term loans (and converted short-term loans)	
2. Pay department overhead	
3. Pay rental costs	
Total outgoing end of year	
NEEDS/DECISIONS	
New long-term loans	
Ending cash balance (for the year)	

The need for new loans and factoring, and the sale of properties, is based on the planned estimated cash flow as shown above.

Decisions

The finance manager is also responsible for closing the books each year.

2.2 Financial Analysis

When we discussed methods for analyzing annual report data we stressed the difficulty of comparison. Financial performance is relative for companies as well as for individuals. Key indicators, such as gross margin as % of sales, can be very helpful in determining your company's progress.

For a restaurant, a profit of one million dollars is probably very high, while for an oil company it is very low. Even within a single industry the variations can be great. One way of getting more information out of a company's financial statements is to use ratio analysis. This involves selecting two figures from a financial statement and expressing the relation between them as a percentage or ratio.

There are four types of ratios:

1. Profitability ratios
2. Leverage ratios
3. Liquidity ratios
4. Turnover ratios

In figure 2.2.1. we list the principal ratios of each type.

Profitability ratios

Profitability ratios show how profitable the company is. Income in relation to assets, equity or sales says more about the company than just the volume of assets, equity or sales. It indicates how much profit has been generated by the resources utilized. If large volumes of assets are not efficiently used, this test will reveal that fact. Price/Earnings ratios and earnings per share are indicators that are used frequently in stock market contexts.

Leverage ratios

Leverage ratios show the company's financial strength. The equity ratio tells us whether the company's assets are owned by the shareholders or by creditors. The Times Interest Earned ratio shows whether the company is so leveraged that its income does not cover interest payments. Liabilities over Assets indicates whether the company can pay its debts. The Debt/Equity ratio shows how the company is financing its activities (debt or equity financing). Equity and Long-term Debt over Total Assets is a broad measure of long-term liabilities (equity is a liability to the

Ratios

Ratio	Numerator	Denominator
Profitability ratios:		
Gross profit margin	Gross profit after product cost	Total Sales
Return on Investment (Assets) ROI	Income before extraordinary items and interest expenses	Total Assets
Return on Equity	Income after financial items and taxes	Average Equity including untaxed reserves less deferred tax liability
Return on Sales	Income before extraordinary items and interest expenses	Total Sales
Price/Earnings Ratio (P/E-Ratio)	Share market price	Earnings per share
Earnings per share EPS	Income before allocations but after adjusted taxes	Number of Shares
Leverage ratios:		
Equity Ratio	Adjusted Equity (Equity plus reserves minus incurred tax debt)	Total Assets
Time Interest Earned	Adjusted income before taxes and interest expenses	Interest Expenses
Ratio of total liabilities to total assets	Total Liabilities	Total Assets
Debt/Equity Ratio	Total Liabilities	Equity
Ratio of capital employed to total assets	Equity and Long-term Debt	Total Assets
Liquidity ratios:		
Quick Ratio (Acid-test Ratio)	Quick Assets	Total Current Liabilities
Current Ratio	Total current Assets	Total Current Liabilities
Turnover ratios:		
Average collection period of receivables	365 X average accounts receivable	Total Sales
Investment (Asset) Turnover	Net Sales	Total Investment (Assets)
Receivables Turnover	Net Sales on Account	Average Net Accounts Receivable
Inventory Turnover	Cost of Goods Sold or Total Sales	Average Inventory or Inventory at Sales Prices

Figure 2.2.1

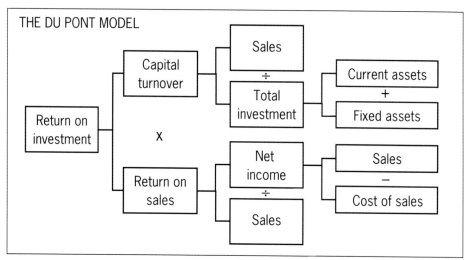

Figure 2.2.2. *The Du Pont model.*

shareholders) over assets. If liabilities are greater than assets the company is financially very weak or may even be bankrupt, depending on the law.

Liquidity ratios

Liquidity ratios indicate solvency and are more short-term in nature than leverage ratios. The basic question they try to answer is whether the company has enough liquid assets to cover its short-term liabilities.

Turnover ratios

Turnover ratios can be said to show how fast resources flow through a company. The higher the turnover, the better, whether we're talking about total capital, inventory or other assets. Low turnover ratios probably indicate that resources are "sleeping" or that the

company's organization is less than optimal. If you look at turnover as "resources generating income," it is obvious that high turnover provides two benefits: higher income and lower capital costs. In fact, increasing turnover ratios has become a movement in the manufacturing industry, called "capital rationalization," which is analogous to the "cost rationalization" efforts generally used in industry.

By now the attentive reader will have seen that there is a link between profit and turnover. Indeed, what was originally a budgeting scheme invented by DuPont & Nemours several decades ago as an aid in introducing divisionalization in the company, has become a widely used model for profitability analysis. It is shown in figure 2.2.2.

This model is very useful for monitoring, budgeting, and directing a company in accordance with an established strategy. If your return on investment (ROI) is low you can backtrack and identify the source of the problem, e.g. low capital turnover. However, too much emphasis on ROI, which stresses current sales and capital utilization, may overshadow the company's long-term goals. For example, the current return on capital might have to be sacrificed in order to cope with investments for future expansion.

In Decision Base the Dupont Model is presented in a slightly different way. There the return on investment is presented as an absolute number rather than as a ratio. For internal monitoring absolute figures can be used, but before any comparisons with other firms or industries can be made, the figures must be converted to ratios first.

What key indicators are really interesting?

What are the key issues in your company?

It depends on your company's operations. Here are some examples: If you can produce a diversity of products with your resources, gross profit margin is obviously a key for decision making. If your job is to develop new products at a high rate, set a high minimum target for gross profit margin and you'll see how your company's profitability will improve in a few years.

If you are a trader or distributor, gross profit margin will also be a key indicator, but the inventory turnover rate is just as important.

If you have a manufacturing operation, the inventory turnover rate may offer the greatest potential for rationalization. If you are in the business of purchasing companies, the P/E ratio for shares will be a key indicator.

Return on investment (ROI) is important in all industries where the demand for operating capital is high, such as manufacturing, processing industries, etc.

It can also depend on your company's particular situation: When you need to borrow money, the bank will be most interested in the Equity ratio or the Debt/Equity ratio.

Time Interest Earned became a key indicator in the period when "high leverage" (controlling as much total capital as possible with as little equity as possible) was considered the smart thing to do.

DECISION BASE ILLUSTRATION: You'll note several of the key indicators indirectly.

The order cards will give you an idea of the gross profit margin for products and markets.

During the year you'll notice how liquidity is consumed by short-term payments for materials, production costs and investments (payments to suppliers). In some instances you'll notice the relative "non-liquidity" of accounts receivable, and definitely that of unsold products, which is precisely the difference between the Current liquidity ratio and the "Acid test."

When you prepare the Profit & Loss Statement you'll notice the sensitive balance between the total contribution margin and general expenses, especially when you have investment programs for new markets or products. You'll notice how interest costs swallow your remaining profit.

The Balance Sheet gives you an idea of the Debt/Equity situation as well as the equity situation itself.

You can thus practice calculating all important key indicators, and discussing the performance and financial position of your company.

When studying ratios one should look at the same ratio over a number of years to see changes in the company's performance. Trends and breaks should be analyzed carefully. Comparisons with other companies, with the industry average or with other countries will show how well the company is doing in relation to its competitors. But different accounting regulations, tax laws, and other factors can result in differences that are not necessarily related to performance.

THINK ABOUT:

- What ratios you would monitor in your company?

- What ratios you would look at if you were a banker evaluating a loan application?

- What you can do to increase inventory turnover?

2.3 Break-Even Analysis

If the ROI stresses the relation between profit, sales and capital turnover, the break-even analysis emphasizes the relation between profits, sales volume and costs. With this analysis you can determine how changes in costs and sales volume will affect profits.

In figure 2.3.1. we can see Alpha's break-even analysis for 1986. The average price a Master series can command is 4.5 M. Alpha's fixed costs include overhead (8 M), marketing (1 M), and interest (2 M). Let's assume that the depreciation is zero. Variable costs are raw materials and production costs - 2 M per series. If Alpha produces 4.5 Master series the total cost will be approximately 20 M. The total revenue on sales of 4.5 Master series will be 20 M.

The break-even point i.e. the point at which total revenue is equal to total cost is thus 4.5 series. This means that Alpha has to sell at least 5 Master series just to cover its fixed and variable costs. Sales volumes below the break-even point will produce a loss while sales volumes above it will result in a profit.

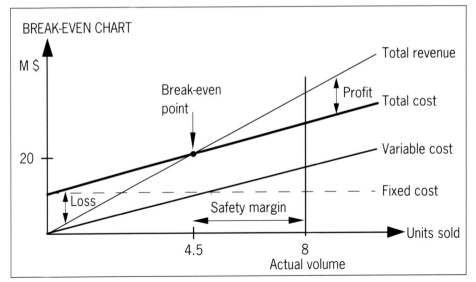

Figure 2.3.1. *Alpha's break-even analysis for 1986*

Estimating sensitivity

The break-even analysis in graphic form is highly valuable for planning. You can immediately see what minimum volume is required, and what safety margin your plan provides, i.e. how much volume you can afford to lose before problems start to arise. You can also perform simulations easily, to see how changes in prices, fixed costs or variable costs affect the break-even point, and how sensitive your business is to such changes. In Alpha's case the actual volume sold in 1986 was eight series. The safety margin is shown in the graph.

The two graphs below present two different cost strategies.

In the case shown on the left, the company has avoided heavy investments and high fixed costs. Instead it has relatively high variable costs. As you can see, we reach the break-even point quickly, because the price level is higher than variable costs, but the profit margin rises rather slowly as the number of units sold increases. This strategy is highly insensitive to volume variations. In other words, the company has decided to play it safe.

In the case presented on the right the company has developed good economies of scale through costly investments that have resulted in extremely low variable costs. The break-even point is thus higher, but above this point the profit margin rises rapidly as the number of units sold increases. You have to keep the volume high however, because you can sustain disastrous losses if you drop below the break-even point. This is a higher-risk strategy.

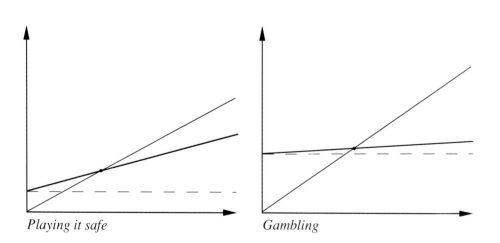

Playing it safe   *Gambling*

Fixed costs and variable costs

Of the many types of costs, some remain fairly constant, regardless of the volume produced. For simplicity we consider them fixed, at least in the short term. Switching to a different production system will change your fixed costs, but merely increasing or decreasing the volume produced will not. Examples of costs we regard as fixed are rental, leasing or capital costs on plant and equipment, overhead, insurance premiums, heating costs, etc. The sum of all of these costs can also be called the company's capacity cost.

Variable costs on the other hand are those that are obviously related to the number of units produced. Costs of materials, components, etc. are variable costs. Salaries and wages directly related to production are usually considered variable costs, at least in a product cost estimate.

There may be some doubt as to whether costs should be classified as fixed or variable. Plant and equipment costs can rise stepwise along with volume. Salaries may be considered fixed if the personnel cannot be laid off. Fixed costs change over time. Actually, it would perhaps be better to regard variable costs as "sunk costs" if the time period involved is very short. An example of such costs are materials purchased for a specific job, and for which

there is no alternative use. In fact we can argue that all costs are fixed in a short-term perspective and that no costs are fixed in a long-term perspective, but such concepts are outside the scope of the break-even analysis.

For practical purposes we assume that some costs are fixed and that others are proportional to the volume produced. If this is obviously the case, we also allow some fixed costs to change stepwise in the graph.

DECISION BASE ILLUSTRATION: If you've decided to plan carefully for the coming year, a break-even analysis can add a degree of sophistication to your planning. The analysis should be performed after the production manager has issued the delivery capacity figures, but before the marketing manager goes to the market. Regard general expenses, depreciation and interest as fixed costs, and material and production costs as variable costs. Estimating revenues can be a problem, because the prices of the various products differ from one another. Estimate an average price and an average cost per series and draw the graph. Indicate your capacity in units to show what your maximum profit can be. The graph now illustrates the business situation, and thus enables you to decide with greater accuracy which orders to accept.

THINK ABOUT:

- What questions a break-even analysis could help your company to answer.

- What you would do if revenues do not cover fixed and variable costs.

- What you would do if revenues do not even cover fixed costs.

- How you could turn some fixed costs into variable costs.

2.4 Capital Budgeting

What should you invest in? How do you choose between alternative investment opportunities? There are some useful methods, often referred to as capital budgeting techniques, for evaluating investments.

An investment that lies within the framework of a company's strategy and that pays back more than it costs is generally considered good for the company. Due to financial and other limitations, a company always has to make choices. And when a company does decide to make a certain invest-ment, there are often alternative ways of going about it, so we need sound methods for comparing the available alternatives.

Basic cash flow model for evaluating investments

All of the cash flow requirements of an investment project must be taken into account in the formulation of an invest-

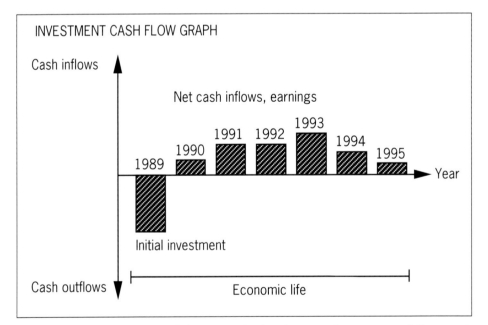

Figure 2.4.1. *It is always a good idea to start by drawing up an investment cash flow graph as shown in this figure.*

ment cash flow chart, in order to evaluate the project correctly and thus determine how the investment should be financed. The items to be determined are initial expenses, annual earnings, economic lifetime, and liquidation costs.

Now let's look at the capital budgeting techniques.

1. Pay-Off Method

A project's pay-off time is simply the number of years it takes to recover the initial cash outlay for the project. The investment alternative with the shortest pay-off time would be the one to choose.

Look at the example in figure 2.4.2.

To calculate the pay-off time we divide the initial investment cost (28

M) by the annual earnings (15 M). The answer is 1.9 years. It takes just under two years for the project to pay for its initial costs. Any revenue beyond that point, any economic life beyond 1.9 years, is profit to the company. We can easily see that this method is biased in favor of projects with high initial earnings. With the pay-off method we might reject projects with a longer economic life and higher total earnings, because this method fails to take cash flows after the pay-off time into account.

The pay-off method can be used as a preliminary check of the alternatives, but a consistent long-term investment strategy must be based on more sophisticated investment calculations.

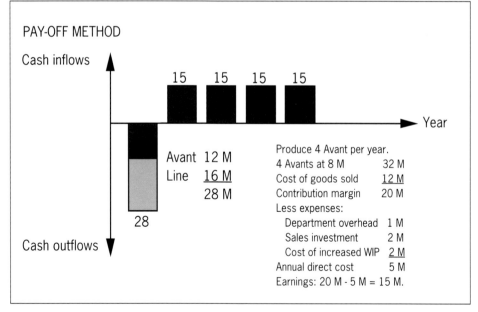

Figure 2.4.2. *The pay-off period for a project is simply the number of years it takes to recover the initial cash outlay for a project.*

2. The Accounting Rate of Return

The accounting rate of return is the average after-tax profit divided by the initial cash outlay. It is quite similar to the return on investment (ROI) see page 67. Using this method as the sole criterion for investment decisions would not be advisable, because it is based on net income instead of cash flows and it does not consider the time factor in the value of money.

3. Net Present Value Method

Net present value (NPV) is a key concept in economic theory. The first thing to understand is that a dollar today is worth more than a dollar tomorrow. Inflation and consumer preferences usually confirm the validity of this statement. Increases in the cost of living gradually reduce the dollar's purchasing power. In general, consumers prefer to consume today rather than tomorrow, which mean that the subjective value of a dollar today is higher than that of tomorrow's dollar. The rate of change in the "perceived" value of a dollar from today to tomorrow is called the discount rate. For example, if the current inflation rate is ten percent, a dollar earned a year from now is worth only 90 cents today.

As we can see, inflation yields an economic discount rate, and consumer preferences yield a subjective discount rate. The greatest difficulty here is deciding which discount rate to use. We must discount all future income flows related to the investment in order to find the net present value, and because the discount rate used obviously determines the net present value, it is highly important.

A widely-used discount rate is the interest rate on bank deposits or treasury bonds. This rate is used because it indicates how much the money would have earned if it had not been invested. Such a discount rate describes the opportunity cost of capital, i.e. the income you lose by not doing what you usually do.

Net present value formula

$$NPV = -C_0 + \frac{\Sigma \, C_t}{(1+r)^t}$$

Where C_0 = initial investment

Σ = the sum of

C_t = expected revenue for each period t

r = discount rate

t = period (year)

Figure 2.4.3. *Formula for the NPV method.*

Project evaluation using the pay-off and NPV methods

Project	c_0	c_1	c_2	c_3	Pay-off	NPV
Avant + Line	-28	15	15	15	1.9	9.3
Excel + Line	-28	15	25	30	1.6	28.8
Optima + Line	-36	0	40	70	1.9	49.6[1]

$$^{1)}\ NPV = -36 + \left(\frac{0}{1.1} + \frac{40}{1.21} + \frac{70}{1.331} \right) = 49.6 \text{ at a discount rate of 10\%.}$$

Figure 2.4.4. *Here you can see how the projects compare, using the pay-off method and the net present value method.*

Consider three alternative investment projects: to develop Avant and a Line, Excel and a Line, or Optima and a Line. To simplify things we assume an economic life of three years. Avant generates a stable income flow. Excel shows a slight increase in earnings over its lifetime. Optima is a slow starter but picks up tremendously towards the end. Let's look at figure 2.4.4. to see how the projects compare, using the pay-off method and the net present value method.

In this example you can see that the pay-off method recommends the Excel alternative, while the NPV method shows that the Optima alternative is much more valuable. If your NPV calculation takes all relevant factors into account and you apply the discount rate in a reasonable way (cost of capital or the possible income resulting from an alternative capital use), you can get a fairly accurate idea of the respective values of the projects by ranking them according to NPV. You can then carry out as many projects as you can afford.

But remember that you cannot compare apples and oranges: A strategic product development project cannot be compared with a production rationalization project purely on the basis of calculations. In addition, NPV calculations cannot be used to compare the value of replacing a machine with that of continuing to use the old machine during the next period. (The method used for this is called the annuity method).

For comparing different investment alternatives, however, the NPV method is quite suitable.

4. Internal Rate of Return Method

The internal rate of return (IRR) on a project is defined as the discount rate that equalizes the present value of cash outflows and inflows. In other words, it is the rate that gives a computed NPV of zero. IRR is the rate of return on invested capital that the project gives the firm. You can find the IRR for a project by trial and error.

In the example presented above, the projects would show the following IRR values:

Avant 28%

Excel 55%

Optima 54%

So the choice between Optima and Excel would depend on your strategy, the size of the projects you can afford and the pay-off time you can afford to wait for.

Using the IRR criterion for investment decisions, we can accept any project that has an IRR greater than the opportunity cost of capital. A company may not be satisfied if it uses the bank deposit rate as the opportunity cost of capital. Instead an internally established profitability rate can be used to better reflect the company's opportunity cost of capital. A firm in a certain industry may know that it needs a 15% return on investments. Another company in another industry may require 25%. The profitability rate needed depends on the nature of the investment and of the industry. A computer manufacturer might require a return of around 40% on a new computer model because it will soon be obsolete. The investments of industries that are less affected by technological change may have a longer economic life, so a lower rate of return may be sufficient. The importance of selecting the discount rate intelligently cannot be overemphasized. It has to reflect the reality of the company and its environments. A carelessly chosen discount rate can do more harm than good. Using the IRR criterion you can accept a project if the discount rate that equates the present value of all cash inflows to that of all cash outflows is higher than the discount rate the firm has established internally.

THINK ABOUT:

- What your company should use as an internal rate of return.

- How you would organize the tasks of project identification and project evaluation in your company.

- How computers can facilitate investment decisions.

2.5 Capital Rationalization

The central idea in the Du Pont model we studied in the section on ratio analysis is that profitability can be increased in two basic ways: 1. By increasing the return on sales. 2. By increasing the capital turnover rate.

There are only two options available for a manager wishing to increase the return on sales: cutting costs or raising prices. But to improve profitability it can be equally interesting to see how capital is tied up in the company. The formula for profitability (return on capital employed) is

$$ROCE = \frac{Profit}{Capital\ employed}$$

This formula can also be expressed as follows:

$$ROCE = \frac{Profit}{Sales} \times \frac{Sales}{Capital\ employed}$$

i.e. ROCE = PROFIT MARGIN x CAPITAL TURNOVER RATE.

Like cost rationalization, which is used to increase profit margins, capital rationalization is used to improve the capital turnover rate. But how can we do this?

In Decision Base the problems of low capital utilization are easy to visualize: There is a logjam of cost carriers in the stocks of materials, stocks of finished products, and accounts receivable areas. We can actually see the money sitting there doing nothing. Unfortunately, few companies are that transparent. Instead we have to study the books and the indicators in order to spot bottlenecks. Experience will also point out likely trouble spots. Take our plate heat exchanger manufacturing company, for instance.

Capital in the production process

The production process is an area of vital importance. A slow production process will cause problems not only in production but also in stocks of materials and accounts receivable. Ordered materials cannot enter production fast enough, so the volumes produced are lower and sales and accounts receivable decline. Congestion in stocks of materials can also be caused by an ordering process that is out of step with production and sales. The production process has to be carefully planned and coordinated with other departments in the company: investment, marketing, etc. Suppose Delta invests in Optima. This new product is "the ultimate in heat exchangers" and it is expensive in terms of cost of materials. Naturally this decision must be followed by another one about which production system is most suitable for Optima. A slow (albeit flexible) production system (job shop) would mean large amounts of tied-up capital (work in process) and relatively limited capacity. If market demand does not constitute a limitation and the product does not require a highly

flexible production system, the most desirable characteristics would be minimum throughput time and maximum capacity.

On the other hand, if Beta is hanging on to Master as a stopgap product until the research for Excel or Optima has been completed, it might make more sense to keep producing Master in job shops. This would provide flexibility, if not high productivity. But assume that Beta's marketing department is going all out to sell Master. If the marketing people fail to coordinate their efforts with production, the company may accept more orders than it can produce. A large old factory with three job shops and one flow shop has an annual capacity of 6 series and costs 4 M in department overhead (in addition to the 20 M tied up in the building itself). The small

Production capacity

Department (prod. unit)	Product	I	II	III	IV	Σ
A: Job shop	Master			1		1.3
B: Job shop	Master			1		1.3
C: Flow shop	Avant		1		1	2.0
D: Line	Excel	1	1	1	1	4.0
E: Line	Optima	1	1	1	1	4.0
F: Line	Optima	1	1	1	1	4.0

Figure 2.5.1 *shows one way to plan production capacity.*

factory with two lines has an annual capacity of eight series, and the department overhead is 50% lower.

Figure 2.5.1. shows one way to plan production capacity. Dates for completion of investments can be included. To reduce the number of errors your company commits in the marketplace, plan carefully and make sure that you provide the marketing department with this information.

Finished products and accounts receivable

Congestion in the stocks of finished products indicates a lack of coordination between production and sales. For some reason the marketing people have been unable to capture enough orders to keep the company operating near full capacity. Perhaps the marketing people were unaware of some extra production capacity. Perhaps the sales effort was insufficient to overcome the competition. An overstocked company needs to ask itself whether its strategy is being followed, whether the budgeted resources are sufficient for achieving the established goals, whether company departments are cooperating, whether information is reaching the right people, whether competition is stiffer than expected, whether quality and service standards are being met, whether...

Accounts receivable are a common source of worry to many companies. Large accounts receivable and little cash look good on the Balance Sheet but may cause problems when bills fall due. A habit of allowing clients to pay late may improve relations, but it certainly hurts capital turnover. Until the customer pays all we can do is wait, unable to put the money to use. However, with accounts receivable in the pipeline, banks will be more inclined to grant a loan.

In order to find out how generous you can be when it comes to payment terms, you have to know how soon you'll need the cash. Here too, cash flow budgets demonstrate their value. A cash flow budget starts with the opening cash balance and then budgets inflows and outflows per week, month, quarter, or any relevant period. In Decision Base especially it is important not to forget year-end expenses such as marketing costs, interest payments, etc. There are periods when outflows tend to be unusually heavy - when taxes, rents and interest payments fall due, for instance. It might be a good idea to grant customer credits up to the dates when considerable outflows are to take place. On the other hand, accepting a long delay in payment on an order will increase outflows, because the cash will come in much later. The cash flow budget shows you whether you can afford it.

Investments

Investments draw a lot of capital. We obviously try to rationalize our inventory capital to the greatest extent possible, but we also try to find the most profitable investments, such as sophisticated production systems that provide good economies of scale. This is not as strange as it may seem. Modern, high-tech production systems reduce product costs more than they increase the cost of capital, and the reduction in the volume of work in process is often far greater than the investment itself. Moreover, if you can shorten the throughput time sufficiently, you can base your plans on customer orders instead of forecasts - and this has far-reaching implications.

THINK ABOUT:

- How your company can increase its capital turnover rate.

- What you should look for in the books to identify a low capital turnover rate.

- A common factor in capital underutilization in a service company.

PART 3.

Planning

3.1 Strategic Planning

Strategic planning is the long-range process used to define and achieve the organization's goals. It is also the process of analyzing major changes in the business environment and understanding structural trends in the industry in which the company operates. This strategic planning will result in actions and activities that strengthen the company's position.

Analyzing the business environment

In general, everything a company does depends on its strategy, which means that managers will have their company's fate in their own hands if they keep abreast of the changes in the business environment, adapt to them, estimate realistically the company's role in the industry and act to take advantage of business opportunities. When structural changes of a revolutionary nature take place, it may be impossible to prevent a company from going under, but it is a shame when this happens simply because of careless strategic planning on the part of managers. The goal should be to surf on the tides of change, to use change to the company's advantage.

Your Decision Base company forms part of the engineering industry, so let's look at a few of the major changes that are relevant here.

1950-1970 was a period of expand-ing production and productivity, when the purchasing power of consumers in the industrial world grew enormously. In the 60s the number of companies competing in most areas was large and companies tended to diversify their product lines to create as many opportunities as possible.

In the 70s changes in the political situation with regard to oil hit heavy industries, steel and shipbuilding. This was also when the Japanese became major players in world industry. In fact, some heat exchanger production had to be moved to Japan because that was where ships were being built. The development of electronics led to major new opportunities in product development and production technology. Companies ceased to diversify and instead opted for developing more sophisticated products and customer values. Some of the most profitable business ideas that emerged during the 70s were based on "total quality" and "service" concepts that obliged companies to increase their levels of refinement. The automotive industry led the way in establishing subcontractor networks, in order to separate manufacturing from assembly. The car manufacturer thus became the developer, assembler and marketer of the product.

In the 80s the trend was concentration; big industries got bigger. Economy of scale became a major necessity as new technologies that demanded extremely heavy and capital intensive investment were introduced. Companies' refinement levels tended to decrease as components and system units became more sophisticated. Consider for example how the diversified computer terminal industry contracted when the PC was launched, and how the production of PCs was then concentrated in Taiwan and a few other places. In every major product area the number of competing companies dropped. Today many world market industries have only four or five competitors. The trend for subcontractors is similar. Subcontractors are getting bigger: it is not unusual for a component supplier to have a world market share of 20%, and to be bigger than the industries it serves. On top of this, strategic alliances between large suppliers are becoming increasingly common, to facilitate the development of subsystems. In the face of such developments, the outlook for

smaller companies is bleak. There is little place for the traditional local subcontractor. Small engineering companies will have to specialize in something rather unique - by becoming OEM suppliers, etc. Operating as a partner in a network of companies will be common, but this will require specialization and a role in the refinement chain of a product type.

This may seem like a more or less fixed situation that offers little margin for action, but understanding our company's business environment will make our strategic planning meaningful. Organizational goals must be developed.

Purpose, mission and objectives

We can break organizational goals down into purpose, mission and objectives. A company's purpose is the role it believes it plays in society. For example Nestlé's purpose could be to fight world hunger, IKEA's purpose could be to provide the world with furniture. A company's mission is narrower, and can be described in terms of products and markets, or the services given and the clients served. Companies within the same industry may have the same purpose but use different means to achieve it, i.e. a different way of describing their mission.

The terms "business mission" and "business idea" are fairly synonymous. They describe the recipe for success -

the combination of opportunities in the business environment and the strength of the company's resources. In a competitive situation the business idea would have these ingredients:

- Who the customer is - market segment, region, application, etc.
- How the customer expresses the needs that we are attempting to satisfy.
- The product/service package that we offer to do this.
- What our specific competitive edges in this area are.
- What basis there is for profitability.

An objective is a specific target expressed in concrete, measurable terms. A company can have several targets, such as becoming market leader, providing better after-sales service, increasing research and development, and reducing production costs.

Strategic planning - doing the right things

Once the company's purpose and mission have been determined, the strategic planning can start. This process is used to develop and maintain a strategic match between the company's expertise and changing market opportunities. Strategic planning differs from operational planning in that the latter is carried out at operational levels and focuses on the current business situation, problems and profitability. We can say that operational planning deals with efficiency - doing things right, while strategic planning concentrates on long-term survival and development, future opportunities and future profits. Here we focus on effectiveness - doing the right things. A company obviously needs both types of planning. If operational planning is overemphasized, the company will have an adaptive type of strategy - a non-strategy of "muddling through," of reacting to situations as they arise.

Strategic dilemmas and opportunities

Some companies have been criticized for concentrating too much on long-term strategy. Critics say that such companies are dull and may miss short-term opportunities. However, today's upswing in hostile takeovers and leveraged buyouts indicates what can happen when strategic planning is neglected. It is often companies that have not adapted to changes, that are stuck with underperforming assets or that have diversified in many different directions that are taken over. The new owners keep the core business and sell off the rest, which seems to indicate that a company is better protected against unfriendly bids if it sticks to what it does best. By growing only in areas close to their core business, firms like Heinz and Sara Lee (both food companies) have managed to deliver high returns to shareholders as well as satisfaction for their managers. In the end, the only defense against a takeover bid is a share price higher than bidders want to pay.

One dilemma for managers is what to do when the business matures, i.e. when it produces a reliable and abundant flow of cash but not much growth or effervescence. They can't just sit and wait for the cash cow to die. The business has to develop. Even within a core business it is possible to find new markets. New applications promote growth: new products can be sold to old customers or old products to new customers. Better management and greater responsiveness to cutomer needs can often be achieved. Focusing on profits instead of turnover might be a more recession-proof strategy. One common way to react to maturing markets is to consolidate. Acquisitions make companies bigger and more international, and global operations can provide greater flexibility. If we don't see available opportunities, someone else will.

Here the company has to identify, evaluate, and select strategic alternatives, i.e. carry out strategic decision making. Imagine that we have a vineyard: The vineyard could develop into a dried fruit company, and then into a food company. Alternatively, the vineyard could start producing fine wines, and then become a wholesaler of luxury goods. It is the strategic planning and decision making that determine the company's future.

Frameworks for strategic planning

There are a number of models that can help managers to analyze their business situation and understand which strategic decisions are best.

Growth opportunities

Growth is one of the most common company objectives. Growth opportunities must be identified and included in the strategic plan. There are three basic growth strategies: intensive growth, integrative growth, and diversified growth.

Intensive growth makes sense for a young company and in young markets. Ansoff developed a matrix for generating ideas for intensive growth opportunities, shown in figure 3.1.1. on page 88.

The matrix summarizes the strategic alternatives for a company aiming at intensive growth.

Integrative growth is a good idea if the company can increase its profitability by expanding vertically or horizontally within the industry. A company achives vertical integration when it gains ownership or control of its supply or distribution system. Horizontal integration take place when a company gains ownership or control of some of

GROWTH OPPORTUNITIES

	Existing products	New products
Existing markets	1. Market penetration	2. Product development
New markets	3. Market development	4.Diversifi-cation

Figure 3.1.1. *Ansoff developed a matrix for generating ideas for intensive growth opportunities.*

its competitors.

Diversified growth can be an option for mature companies and markets. Diversification does not mean that the company should grab any opportunity that comes along. Instead, the company should attempt to identify areas where its particular skills are most valuable, or that can help it to overcome a particular problem. It may pay for a jewelry chain to take over a company that provides security services. Such diversification does not exploit the jeweler's skills but is motivated by the fact that the company consumes large amounts of security services.

Product portfolio analysis

Once a company's growth opportunities have been analyzed, management is in a better position to make decisions on the company's product lines. All of the company's current operations must be evaluated, to enable management to make decisions on the development of new products, and on which products to maintain, phase down, or phase out. There are two well-known tools for product portfolio evaluation. The first one presented is the Boston Consulting Group's "Growth-Share Matrix," a four-field model that shows the strategic balance for the various business units of a company. It is reproduced in figure 3.1.2.

This model is based on the assumption that the correlation between

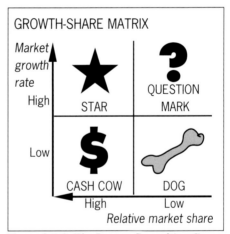

Figure 3.1.2. *The Boston Consulting Group classifies products in a growth-share matrix.*

profit level and market share is high, that the "experience curve" is valid and that cash outflow increases when a company tries to expand along with a rapidly expanding market. On the vertical axis we see the market growth rate. This is the annual growth rate of the market in which the product is located. A low market growth rate can be less than 10% while a high market growth rate can exceed 20%. Relative market share is shown on the horizontal axis. It is the market share of the product relative to that of the industry's largest competitor. A high relative market share can be 3, which means 3 times as strong as the next strongest company. A low relative market share can be 0.1, which means that the product's share amounts to 10% of the market leader's share. By splitting the matrix at 1.0, the point

where the company's market share is equal to that of the biggest competitor, we can divide the chart into four sections that represent four different strategic situations:

- Stars are high-growth, high-share products. They are rising now, but they will eventually slack off and perhaps fall.

- Cash cows are low-growth, high-share products. These products provide the cash the company needs to develop new stars.

- Question marks are low-share, high-growth products. The question is whether management should spend more money to try to capture a greater market share and make the product a star. If not, the product should be phased down or out.

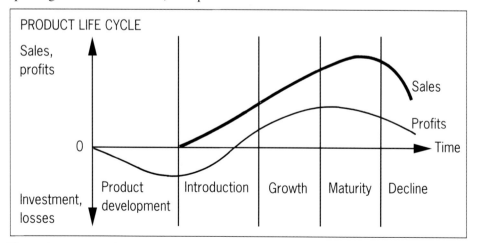

Figure 3.1.3 *shows the consequences of the product life cycle on sales and profits.*

sid 89

- Dogs are low-share, low-growth products. They are cash traps in the sense that they generate cash only for their own maintenance and no more. But if we can develop a market niche that frees the dog from competition, it might become very profitable, in spite of its small share in the industry.

The BCG matrix model assumes that products have life cycles. A product goes through stages of development, introduction, growth, maturity, and decline. A question mark may develop into a star, which can then become a cash cow that lives a long and healthy life before it declines. Figure 3.1.3 shows the consequences of the product life cycle on sales and profits.

The product life cycle theory states that a company has to develop new products continuously in order to stay in business.

The second product portfolio evaluation model is General Electric's strategic business-planning grid. It takes into account the fact that other factors beside market growth and market share enter into the decision-making process.

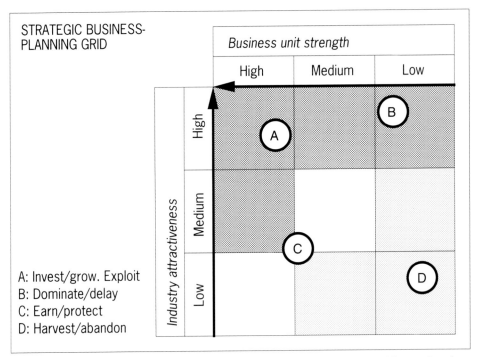

Figure 3.1.4. *General Electric developed its strategic business-planning grid assuming that other factors beside market growth and market share enter into the decision-making process.*

This is shown in figure 3.1.4.

Industry attractiveness is an index made up of factors such as market size, market share, profit margin, and economies of scale. Business unit strength consists of factors such as relative market share, price competitiveness, product quality and after-sales services. The grid represents a combination of market characteristics and the company's competitive position. Clearly the ideal is a product with a high industry attractiveness and high business unit strength. Such products are located in the upper left hand corner of the grid. Products located in the squares on the diagonal from upper right to lower left have shown mediocre performance. Finally, the squares in the lower right-hand corner contain products that should probably be phased out.

Regardless of the method used, a company must evaluate its products in order to set goals and allocate resources. It is then the task of the marketing department to achieve those goals.

Finally, remember that a strategy that does not create or exploit a particular advantage of the company over its rivals should be rejected.

THINK ABOUT:

- How to implement a formal strategic-planning process.
- How to implement the strategy.
- How to measure and control the implementation process.

3.2. Competitor Analysis and Marketing Style

In carrying out their responsibilities for marketing planning, execution, and control, managers need a great deal of information.

Before a company can decide on market segmentation and targeting, it has to analyze the world it is operating in. We will illustrate this with examples from the consumer marketing field.

Business environment

A company is affected by its demographic environment, i.e. population growth, age profile of the population, average level of education and geographical mobility of people. Economic factors such as interest rates, inflation, real income growth, savings patterns, etc. clearly have an impact on business. Environmental concerns will affect the supply of raw materials, cost of energy and levels of pollution. Other areas of equal importance are the company's technological, political, and cultural environments.

A company has to analyze its potential customers. Who has the purchasing power? How are purchasing decisions being made? What influences consumers? Questions like these have to be answered before a marketing plan can be developed.

The competitive situation constitutes yet another component of the company's environment. The company must identify and monitor its competitors in order to gain and hold a profitable share of the market. Now we'll look at ways to analyze the competitive environment.

Competitive analysis

In Decision Base a time usually comes when the participants realize the value of information about competitors' results and plans; the boards are covered up to conceal investment programs. (Interestingly enough, trade in such information does not seem to develop.) However, the competitive environment consists not only of other companies. Seen from the consumer's point of view, the first question is what desire he or she wants to satisfy. In this sense, an ice cream producer faces "substitute competition" from travel agents, depending on how consumers set their priorities. Let's now assume that our consumer wishes to satisfy the desire to eat. The next question is what to eat. Here we find "generic competition." The options are many: eat at a restaurant, grab some fast food, cook at home, buy a TV-dinner or candy, popcorn, ice cream, fruit, etc. If our consumer decides to eat out, we then run into "product competition." Will it be French, Chinese or Indian cousine - or fast food? Finally, choosing a restaurant involves "brand competition." If there are few hamburger restaurants in town, going to McDonald's rather than Burger King involves a choice between brands.

A company that analyzes the competitive market as described will be able to identify all of the competitors that are preventing it from selling more of its product. This information will help management to spot opportunities and will improve the competitive edge of its product over the various substi-

tute generic, product, and brand competitors.

Marketing style

Once we carry out the competitor analysis, we'll probably realize that it's impossible to compete everywhere. Different competitors will be in the best position to serve particular segments of the market. There are basically three marketing styles:

1. Mass marketing: the seller mass-produces and mass-distributes one product to all kinds of buyers. This style does not adapt the product to differences in demand. Rather, the customer has to adapt to the product. Examples of companies employing this marketing style are Coca-Cola, McDonald's and IKEA.

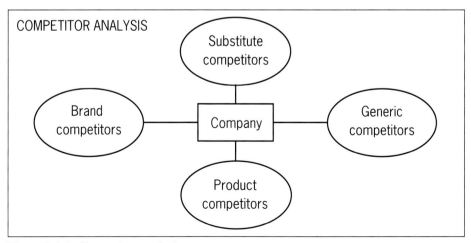

Figure 3.2.1. *Competitor analysis.*

2. Product-differentiated marketing: this style does not quite adapt the product to consumer groups, but it offers them variety. Product differentiation is used by our Decision Base company that develops Avant. The new products are not designed to meet different consumer needs. Instead, product differentiation provides alternatives.

3. Target marketing: the company identifies different groups or segments making up the market. Products and marketing are then modified to match the targeted segment or segments. Diet Coke is aimed at the weight-conscious consumer of soft drinks. Armani clothes developed Mani for people with smaller pocketbooks. In Hong Kong a credit card has been developed for chic housewives.

Marketing the same product worldwide and in the same way in every country is a strategy that has obvious economic appeal. But even the most famous mass-marketed brand-name goods need to be tailored to local markets in order to sell. This can involve altering the image: Schweppes tonic water is advertised as a mixer for alcoholic beverages in Britain, but as a soft drink in France.

Market segmentation or target marketing is perhaps becoming the dominant marketing style. Market segments must be measurable, accessible, and substantial if a company is to be successful. In other words, it must be possible to identify and reach the segment, and the segment must be large enough so that a company can profit by designing a special product or line for it. Because target marketing is expensive, you don't see many cars developed especially for people less than five feet tall. A market can be broken down into segments in various ways: geographically (region, climate, city size), demographically (age, sex, income, occupation, family size), or behavioristically. The latter distinguishes such factors as whether the product is used often or rarely, is cheap or prestigious, appeals to first-time users or regular users, etc. There are of course many other possibilities available to the creative company.

No marketing strategy is always the best. The marketing methods that bring success in one case may often prove disastrous in another. It is interesting to note that around 90% of all new products fail. Today's best selling products were invented a century ago - Coca Cola, Ivory soap, Quaker Oats, etc. Marketing tries to answer two basic questions: Is the product or service something that people want to buy, and what competitive advantage do you have in supplying that product? High rates of product failure also appear to be due to market research problems. Companies still don't know enough about their markets and customers, or they know the wrong things. Common sense and experience remain the core of good marketing. Market research and intelligent use of the information it provides will improve a company's chances of success.

THINK ABOUT:

- How you would conduct a consumer analysis for your company.
- How you would design a marketing program for a product or service of your choice.
- Environmental factors, such as the way the discovery of holes in the ozone layer has affected industries that use CFCs (a gas used in spray cans, refrigerators, etc.)

DECISION BASE ILLUSTRATION: Of course, it would be better if your product/market strategy didn't coincide with your competitors'. At the very least, keep track of the following information:

- Who is present in which market? (This is obviously public knowledge.)

- Who is developing what products and when? (This information is more difficult to obtain during the development stage.)

- Who is developing what production capacity?

The Decision Base market can support four competitors without their recurring to unusually shrewd strategic planning and information systems - but it cannot support six. If your strategy is not smart enough, bankruptcy cannot be excluded from the list of possible scenarios. The Decision Support tools can help you obtain information about the business environment and competitors.

3.3 International Marketing

The interest in and importance of selling in foreign countries varies from one company and country to another.

In large markets like the United States, Japan, Germany, France, etc., a company may be quite satisfied to limit itself to its domestic market. For companies in smaller markets like Scandinavia, the Netherlands, Switzerland, etc. export may be an absolute necessity, for reasons of volume and cost if nothing else. If you feel that your product is highly competitive, you will have a natural incentive to expand into international markets in order to take advantage of the opportunities there.

It may be true that "all business is local," but if you look at the structural changes that have taken place in industries like transport or engineering, you'll most likely find that your customers are internationalized, multinational, multilocal or whatever. If you want to attract them you're going to have to follow them. This is the situation for heat exchanger manufacturers, for instance.

What is the difference between international trading and domestic marketing? To start with, there are currency exchange controls, tariffs, quotas, and all kinds of non-tariff barriers to overcome. Then there are the political, legal, cultural, and other differences that have to be dealt with. In addition, there is the problem of understanding foreign customers' needs, understanding marketing communications norms, finding the market information you need and finding the right market channels, dealing with language barriers and misunderstandings, etc. etc.

These are obvious drawbacks for the foreigner who wants to sell in an export market - drawbacks that give the local supplier a certain advantage - and the drawbacks increase with the remoteness of the market. So you'll have to work hard to create a market position and a local organization, and to make your presence and your USP (unique selling proposition) known. A company that decides to go abroad should first define its international marketing objectives and policies. What proportion of foreign to total sales would be desirable? Should the company concentrate on a few markets or sell in many countries? What types of countries would it be best to trade with?

How to enter a foreign market

The procedure for deciding which markets to enter is relatively straightforward. Current and future market potentials have to be estimated and forecast. Sales, costs, and profits must also be studied, as well as the estimated return on investment. It is usually a good idea to include a risk premium in investment calculations, i.e. to require a higher rate of return on foreign operations than on domestic operations.

There are various ways to establish your company in a foreign market: opening a sales office, setting up a subsidiary, starting a joint venture with a local company, executing a license agreement with a local manufacturer, engaging an agent to conduct business on your behalf or a distributor working on his own account, etc. The choice depends on your strategy and the particular circumstances.

The marketing mix

If your product is of a kind typically made in large-scale production, or if it is a commodity (little differentiation), you have to choose a suitable marketing mix for each market, i.e. the degree to which the marketing program should be adapted to local conditions. The marketing mix (often called the four P's for Product, Price, Promotion and Place) has a number of variables that have to be defined.

For example, should the same product be offered to all markets or should it be modified to respond to different consumer tastes? Campbell soup is quite successful in marketing the same product in different markets while General Foods offers different coffee blends for different tastes. Prices charged in foreign markets are often different from those charged at home, because a product must be priced in accordance with the country's general price level. Perhaps the product has more luxury appeal on a foreign market so a higher price can be charged. Lower prices are often used to capture market share, but be careful! If you set your price below the local production cost you are likely to be accused of dumping and fined, etc., to reduce your competitive edge.

Promotion

The most suitable type of promotion depends on the product's image in the market in question. Lifestyle advertising themes are sometimes standardized internationally. For example, Coca Cola's "Coke is it!" or Apple Computer's "The power to be your best" repeat a suggestive message designed to make the customer feel like a member of the global village. The strategy is to make the customer adapt to the international product. But language and cultural barriers can catch you off guard. In Spanish, Chevrolet's Nova was called no va, which means "it doesn't go." Colors in ads may have to be changed because they convey the wrong message. In Japan for instance, white is a color of mourning.

Normally you would adapt your promotion to the culture of the foreign market and use the media accordingly. What is normal language in American advertising can easily give a negative impression in Europe and vice-versa. The European countries have different cultural styles, which means that Europe cannot be covered with one channel or medium. (Maybe there is no such thing as "European," "American," "Asian" or "African." In Europe the word "Paneuropean" is coming into use.)

Distribution

Place involves not only the choice of market, but also the choice of distribution channels. The first problem to solve is how to get the product from one country to another. But there is more to it than that. Distribution systems within countries and to the consumer vary significantly. In one country it might be possible to work without middlemen, but in another a long and complex distribution chain might be required. Fi-

nally, the company must develop an effective international marketing organization. Most companies start with an export department. When the company's international operations grow more demanding, an international division is usually set up.

"Multidomestic" companies

A few companies go beyond this stage and become multinational, world-wide, organizations. Such companies can view the world from a bird's-eye perspective and feel at home anywhere. They adapt their marketing efforts wherever they go and they operate wherever economic conditions or regulations make it suitable to do so. That is why they call themselves "multidomestic."

International marketing in the Decision Base form

The heat exchanger business forms part of the engineering industry. The product got its start in 19th century dairy technology, which consisted of the separator, the milking machine and the cooler. The latter gradually became the modern heat exchanger. (Ours is of plate type.) Marine applications constitute a large market, and the fact that Sweden used to be the second largest shipbuilding country in the world is one reason why our company became so strong and competitive internationally. The heat exchanger business is thus international in terms of markets, and it is quite possible to develop economies of scale in production, even though each product generation has a great many variants. (Master is not a single product specification; it represents instead a fairly large range of heat exchangers of various sizes - all of them based on the same technology and production method.)

On the domestic market you can limit yourself to a narrow range of Master products suitable for that market, and concentrate on improving your productivity while avoiding any radical development. This strategy will work for a time, but within a few years someone will offer your customers a better product and then they'll leave you.

In Decision Base expansion is normally concentric, which means that it is relatively easy to establish yourself on the Scandinavian market. (Remember that Decision Base originated in Sweden.) The Scandinavian languages and cultures are similar, and even though there are important differences between the basic industries of these countries, Scandinavians understand each another quite well.

Scandinavia is "surrounded" by Europe, which consists of a many large markets that are very demanding but not far away. The assumption here is that you can establish your company, including organization and distributors, within one year, but in reality it takes longer to get acquainted with the markets.

We're sure you won't have any trouble taking the Sweden/Scandinavia/Europe/Overseas/Faraway market setup and converting it to a similar layout centered on your own domestic market. In the real world exporters have to face competition from local manufacturers in most big markets, so they need some technical or cost advantage to compensate for the disadvantages that they as foreigner have. In Decision Base this is simulated by one of the competitors having established himself in a market before you do. By the time you reach the market, this competitor will already be the market leader. Why not look for markets where there are no domestic manufacturers, i.e. no one with a position to defend? (This appears to have been the strategy of Japanese car manufacturers when they first came to Europe. They started in Finland, Ireland, etc., not in Italy and Germany).

So much for "Sweden, Scandinavia and Europe." Establishing yourself overseas demands a great deal more. You may be able to develop a market niche quickly if you have a specialty, but it will take several years to create a real market position. And it takes even longer to get established on the "faraway" market (Asia from the European point of view), because we have to overcome many more cultural barriers and learn to "think Asian."

With a little imagination on your part, Decision Base can give you a good idea of what international marketing is like.

THINK ABOUT:

- Whether agents are a good alternative to direct export.
- When licensing can be better than joint ownership.
- Reasons for direct investment.
- How to conduct a market survey.
- How packaging can be used as promotion and to reduce costs.

3.4 Management Information Systems

In its best form the management information system adds reliability and speed to the company's decision making processes, it enables managers to react in time to important changes and it gives them the freedom to rely on their intuition.

"Management information" is the information used for planning, decision making and control. "Systems" refers to the systematic, preferably computerized, means of collecting, processing, distributing and presenting information to decision makers.

What kind of information is required? To start with, it has to be relevant and as brief as possible, but as complete as necessary. *Internal company information* is required, as well as *outside information* from the business environment. Determining what information is relevant and necessary for a manager at a given time is like peeling the leaves off an artichoke. As the situation emerges, new information needs come to light. Let's see how Decision Base illustrates this.

What specific information is needed?

When running a company in Decision Base you'll find out step by step and in a very natural way what specific information you need in your role as manager.

During the first year you don't really need any management information because everything is determined and no changes are to be made. The first time you do any strategic planning is when you prepare for the second year. The company is then in good financial shape and has several development options. A *trade journal* for the industry is your *source* of market forecasts for various products in different market areas.

The first crucial information you need is internal in nature: the *delivery capacity* of your factory. When you later go to the market, you get an idea of the *market demand*, and you may pay some attention to your *competitors' strategies* and note roughly what they involve. In the beginning there is enough money available, but if your development plan is expansive, money may gradually become a problem. *Liquidity* then becomes a factor and you start doing preliminary calculations to at least find out how much you need to borrow from the bank.

The next thing that becomes evident is that market leadership tends to be one of the key factors for success. Perhaps you then start taking more careful note of *customer enquiries*, and you make a more concerted effort to find out more about your *competitors' investments.*

What's happening to your profit level? After a few years most of your company's equity may have gone into "investments" in new products and market positions. When the pressure on the company's economy increases, you notice that it becomes vital to keep track of the contribution margin on each order, so you start paying closer attention to *market prices*. Soon you'll become aware of signals that indicate *product life cycles*. When you realize that the interest cost of borrowed capital is in fact taking much of your profit, you'll turn your attention inward again. Minimizing the level of capital in the material flow (purchasing, inventory, production, stock) requires detailed control of *orders and capacities*, as well as good cost control. Keeping debt at a minimum at all times requires extremely precise *liquidity planning*. And so on.

When you feel that your company's development has stabilized, you'll start to compare each year's results with those of previous years. You'll check a few suitable *key indicators* in order to make this comparison over time. By the way, it's an excellent idea to awaken interest throughout your organization in the most important key indicators, and to make people aware of them.

At the beginning, your *planning system* may consist of a sheet of paper where you note down only the few items of information that you cannot do without. Once you're under way, you increase the quantity of information, but still limit yourself to those items that seem to be necessary. But gradually, you design your own information processing tools. After a few years you may feel that the work has become unwieldy and that your budgeting precision, for example, should be improved. Then you start to standardize your information tools and formalize the process. Maybe you'll look for a standard management information system that you can use in your company. And it just so happens that your systems supplier has one on hand! It's called "Decision Support" and it may be just what you're looking for. Implementing it will sharpen your planning procedures, increase your precision and speed up your planning.

We believe that it provides a good simulation of the real thing. Note that you start from a position of scarcity, not abundance. When you really feel the need for a piece of information you'll be motivated to search for it, analyze it and create a tool for it.

A general view of management information systems

Before computers became widely available, management had access to much less information that cost more and arrived much later. Data processing has radically changed the working environment for planners and controllers. Information can be generated in different ways. The company itself produces some information, such as annual reports, and it can obtain other information from firms that sell data on markets, products, and issues. Sometimes the information required is very specific so a special study has to be carried out. A company may have a research department and do its own research, or it can commission a research institute to do such work. One serious problem is to determine what information is needed. Managers are often swamped by potentially interesting but basically useless data and information. The challenge is to determine the information requirements and how to meet them, on both the operational and strategic planning levels. The purpose of a management information system is to provide managers with the right information at the right time. However, if the cost of acquiring the information is higher than

the potential savings the information makes possible, then the system is not cost-effective.

It may be difficult to determine a management information system's cost-effectiveness. How do you quantify the value of information? The value of information depends on four factors: the information's quality, timeliness, quantity, and relevance. There is usually a positive correlation between quality and cost. The secret is to know the level of sophistication that is required and not ask for more. Timeliness is crucial. The information must be available in time for action to be taken. Whether information is timely depends on the situation. Strategic planners working on long-term projects may be satisfied with rather infrequent analyses of internal data, but they need quick access to information involving changes in the external environment. People working at the operational level must be provided with internal information and data analysis much more frequently.

Obviously, insufficient information is a problem, though a less expensive one than too much information. It is not only silly to pay for information you do not use, it may also overwhelm managers to such an extent that they overlook important information. The information provided should be relevant to the employee's responsibilities. Personnel managers do not need to know about inventory levels, and other department heads need to know about the status of staff members in their respective departments only.

The designing of a management information system is usually a gradual process. Transaction processing systems are the first to be installed, followed by operational control systems. Systems for decision making are not introduced until later, and strategic planning systems are implemented last. When designing an information system, we have to remember that the information needs of a particular manager depends on his or her position in the company hierarchy. Top-level managers working with strategic planning will use mostly external sources of information that tell them about competitors, economic conditions, etc. Mid-level managers need information from both external and internal sources. They also require a more rapid flow of information. Lower-level managers who work with operational control need frequent, highly detailed, and accurate information. This information can usually be obtained from internal sources.

The MIS dream

Many large companies used to dream about a "total management information system" residing in a central computer. All relevant data would be run through certain data processing routines, and consequences would be automatically calculated. The manager would merely focus on a specific area of interest and the system would provide decision making data instantly. Attempts were made to design such systems but they failed for obvious reasons. People are not machines, the process of producing information is not so straightforward, creativity is not so linear, etc. The most convincing illustration of this was the way the first oil crisis in 1973 took everyone by surprise. Good management information systems should at least have been able to predict something as important as this, but none of them seemed to have done so. Perhaps an "excessively good" information system, like an "excessively good" budgeting system, reduces your flexibility by diminishing your capacity to react to changes and strategic surprises.

The aim of a Management Information System is to increase your preparedness, your flexibility and your ability to take advantage of changes in the business environment.

THINK ABOUT:

- The differences between data, information, and management information.

- What personnel problems you may encounter when implementing a computerized information system.

3.5 Corporate Finance

In Decision Base you quickly discover the need for outside financing. The financial consequences of investment decisions are enormous.

The corporation (limited liability company) is one of the best organizational forms in existence, and it has produced more wealth than perhaps any other. A corporation is a legal entity and is itself responsible for any agreements and arrangements made in its name. It is based on a business idea and on limited equity put up by the original shareholders, and it may obtain all of the outside financing it can attract. The benefit is that, via a corporation, a small number of people can take on projects that would be far beyond their reach as private persons.

Of course there are very strict laws regulating what the owners may do and how the company is to be managed, since no physical person is actually responsible for the company's liabilities to third parties. However, the members of the board of directors can be held personally responsible if they fail to comply with legal regulations related to insider trading, etc. In extreme cases they can go to jail.

The finance department

Financial planning involves the use of funds and sources of funds. Financial decisions deal with the amount of capital required and the financing structure. Some major underlying questions here are:

- How large should the enterprise be and how fast should it grow?
- What specific assets should an enterprise acquire?
- How much working capital is needed?
- How much cash is needed?
- How should the required financing be obtained?

The main financial goal of management is to increase shareholder wealth. This is what the company president is hired for and it is his legal duty. To achieve this primary goal, which is a long-term goal, you have to satisfy your customers and operate the company efficiently. If the value (equity) of a company appears to drop over a certain period of time, a reliable forecast must be carried out to ensure that the drop is actually due to the cost of an investment that will pay off handsomely in the not too distant future.

The objective of the finance department is to arrange the best possible financing (lowest possible capital cost) and to minimize financial risk. The company starts with the share capital as equity and, if the company is profitable, the equity will grow along with after-tax profits. If insufficient equity is available for financing investments and working capital, the company has to borrow money from outside sources. This can give the capital considerable leverage, and enable the company to take on large projects.

Of course the company has to put up some collateral - a mortgage on real property or even a mortgage on the company itself if the bank has confidence in the company. In fact, you can borrow money without any collateral whatsoever if you promise to pay sufficiently high interest. That is the idea behind junk bonds, the "brilliant" financial invention of the 80's. This scheme will work as long as people believe that market values will continue to rise.

Sources of financing

As shown in the illustration, a company has many sources of financing. You can see some of them in Decision Base:

- The share capital, the original new capital issue, amounts to 5 M.

- Accumulated retained earnings including net profit for the year are available from internal sources. (To calculate this you must add back the depreciation that was specified in the Profit & Loss Statement.)

- External sources include long-term bank loans. Accounts payable and advances from customers are not included in the simulation, but you can use short-term bank loans instead.

- For non-balance sheet financing you can use factoring and rent factories. This is similar to leasing.

In real life a company with a good record can issue new shares to increase its equity. In Decision Base this is one of the possibilities we can use to keep a bankrupt company afloat. The bank then converts the loan to share capital.

It is necessary to distinguish between internal and external financing. The equity belongs to the company itself and cannot be reclaimed unless the company is liquidated. It can be paid out to shareholders as dividends, but only that portion that is free and only on an equitable basis and in accordance with an agreement. On the other hand, loans are reclaimed when the contracts expire or when the value of the collateral declines. The stipulated interest has to be paid regardless of whether the company is sufficiently profitable or not. Accounts payable, advances from customers and deferred tax liabilities are normally free from interest costs and are thus highly attractive external sources of financing.

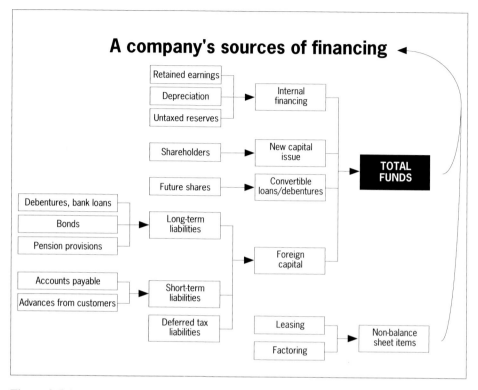

Figure 3.5.1. *A company's sources of financing.*

The way in which a company chooses to finance its operations, and the proportion of debt to equity, are what determine the company's capital structure.

The leverage effect and optimum capital structure

If there are no market limits on the size of your operations and the business is profitable, borrowing money and expanding your operations is the logical thing to do. If profitability is higher than the bank interest rate, the surplus profit goes to equity. The more we borrow the higher the percentage return on equity. This positive leverage makes external financing very attractive.

If the profitability of the business drops below the bank interest rate, the leverage effect obviously turns against you. When this happens you have to sell off assets and reduce your loans quickly. In real life, the higher the interest rate, the higher up on the lever the loan in question is situated. (This is where junk bonds backfire; no assets are provided as collateral in the first place, and interest rates are higher than usual.)

If you keep on borrowing to finance

an unprofitable operation you may eventually land in a debt trap where your interest costs are always higher than your profit level. The important thing to remember here is that it is extremely difficult to earn your way out of a high-debt situation once you've fallen into it.

So the question is what level of leverage is best. Financial risk can be looked upon as a statistical cost, i.e. the cost of bankruptcy multiplied by the probability of bankruptcy. If you have no external capital, you're probably not exploiting your full potential. If you have too much external capital you're taking too big a risk of losing control. So the debt/equity ratio is one of the finance department's most important key indicators.

There seems to be an optimum capital structure which varies depending on the type of business in question. In the type of industry which serves as a model in Decision Base, a debt/equity ratio of 4:1 is accepted by the bank. On equity up to a ratio of 2:1, the bank charges 10% interest and above that it charges 20%. In a retail operation the acceptable D/E ratio can be 6:1 to 8:1, and a bank's or contractor's can be even higher. This depends on substance values, profit levels and risk levels.

Financial goals

The minimum target for return on capital employed has to be based on assump-

tions of the investors' alternatives. Investors can choose between investing in the high-risk stock market, and buying government bonds which are considered risk-free. A company's shareholders should thus be expected to demand a return on their invested capital amounting to the bond interest rate plus a risk premium. (The shareholders' ROI consists of dividends plus the increase in the market value of the shares.) This can serve as a guideline for non-listed companies as well.

A financial goal can also be calculated like this:

Real rate of interest	3 %
+ estimated inflation	8 %
+ preferred risk premium	5 %
= after-tax return on equity	16 %

divided by (1 minus tax rate), say 0.5

= pre-tax return on equity	32 %

Now look at the balance sheet to determine the capital structure. Let's assume that it is similar to the following:

	interest
20 % current liabilities	0 %
40 % bank loans and similar	15 %
20 % untaxed reserves	0 %
20 % equity	32 %
100 % with a capital cost of	12.4 %

(average percentage) before taxes, including the risk premium.

This gives you the minimum return on investment. It obviously depends on

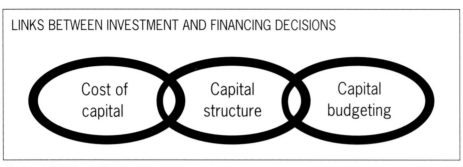

Figure 3.5.2. *Links between investment and financing decisions.*

the current tax rate, estimated inflation and the average cost of total capital which, in turn, depends on the capital structure.

As the discussion above indicates, we cannot separate investment decisions from financing decisions. A leveraged firm will have higher capital costs, and will thus have to impose higher rates of return on its investment projects. And the firm's investment and capital structure is what determines its value on the stock market. Clearly, a firm's debt policy matters.

Changes in capital structure and dividend policy also send signals to the stock market. Generally such signals are correct. An increase in dividend payouts signals that the firm expects permanently higher cash flows in the long term. Unsuccessful firms will not have sufficient cash flow to back up such signals if they attempt to fool the market. Furthermore, managers have an incentive to tell the truth in order to keep their jobs and avoid prosecution. The cases of insider trading brought to court in the past few years probably also encourage managers to stick to the truth.

The capital structure of a firm will depend on its history. For example, a very profitable firm in an industry with relatively slow growth will end up with an unusually low debt/equity ratio. An unprofitable firm in the same industry will end up with a high D/E ratio.

A firm can actually have too much cash. Too much cash depresses the return on capital and results in sluggish share prices. At times the situation can appear to be absurd: IBM had record profits one year in the 70's, and this led to a drop in the share price on the stock market. The reason was that investors assumed that IBM would not be capable of investing so much cash in anything as profitable as its current operations. This in turn can make companies vulnerable to takeovers.

Takeovers and other practices

Low share prices make it possible for managers and venture capitalists to take public companies private. If the shares are paid for with borrowed money it is called a leveraged buyout. The benefits of such takeovers are the elimination of shareholders' servicing costs, better management, and an incentive (the increased leverage) to cut the fat from operating costs. Such takeovers have become quite common in recent years. Between 1984 and 1988 American managers exchanged equity for more than $212 billion of debt to take public companies private. Not all countries think that the takeover craze is a good thing. In Switzerland there are regulations that protect Swiss companies from hostile takeovers. America's wave of debt-financed takeovers has reached Britain. British non-financial firms have a relatively low debt/equity ratio, which makes them ideal targets for leveraged buyouts. However, comparing debt levels internationally is no easy task. International differences may reflect institutional arrangements rather than financial prudence. Companies in Japan and Germany may be able to support a higher amount of debt because banks there hold sizable equity stakes in non-financial firms and are often represented on company boards. This reduces the incentive for banks to force bankruptcy. So even if American and British companies can afford more debt, it would be risky for them to approach Japanese or German debt levels.

THINK ABOUT:

- Reasons why the value of a firm may differ from the price the company's stock would command on the stock market.

- Does it make any difference to shareholders whether profits are reinvested or distributed as dividends?

- How to determine the optimum capital structure for your company.

3.6 Case Study 1: How Beta approached the 90s

Beta is a company that produces plate heat exchangers. Its new management is challenged to develop a strategy for the company.

The management believes that the adaptive type of strategy-making the company has employed up until now is highly unsuitable in a rapidly changing environment.

The first thing the management team does is to analyze the current situation. Consultants tell them that more technically advanced plate heat exchangers will be in demand in the future. The simple technology used to produce Master type plate heat exchangers will be copied by manufacturers benefiting from low labor costs, so price competition will become tougher.

In the domestic market Beta has five competitors. They have all reached maturity in the market and face the same need to revitalize their companies.

We let Beta's managing director continue:

"Our strengths and weaknesses had to be identified. We found that our technical skills were high enough to enable new products and new production methods to be developed and installed within a few years. This was an asset to exploit. Research and development along with investments in machinery and equipment require a lot of cash. As a result of our company's financial strength, we didn't have to worry about bank relations. The suppliers we worked with were reliable and flexible enough to work on a just-in-time basis. Our customer relations were excellent, due in large part to the high quality of our products.

On the other hand we considered our reliance on the domestic market a potential problem. Manufacturing just one product increased our vulnerability further. With growing competition our profit margins would certainly shrink.

The production process we used was very slow and tied up considerable amounts of capital. In 1985 the capital turnover rate was an appalling 0.43. We realized that we were paying too high a price for flexibility."

What Beta's manager told us can be summarized as follows:

Strengths:
- Technical skills
- Financial strength

- Access to new technology
- Reliable suppliers
- High-quality products

Weaknesses:

- Weak market position
- Old-fashioned production methods
- Few products
- High level of tied-up capital
- Low capacity utilization

The next step Beta managers take is to identify available opportunities. They hire consultants, do a great deal of research and finally come up with three possible new products and four possible new markets. The products are Avant, Excel and Optima, and the markets are Scandinavia, Europe, North America and Asia.

Similar analysis enables management to come to the conclusion that Avant is almost a direct substitute for Master, Excel will initially do better in the richer markets, and Optima is the product for the high-tech niche and for the very long term.

The products can be placed in submarkets of their own on the basis of their flexibility and the technology used. This is shown in figure 3.6.2.

The entire market for plate heat exchangers was also studied. The consultants report the following:

"The introduction of more advanced products on the market will lead to a higher world demand for plate heat exchangers. The market will show high annual growth well into the 90s. As the market grows, new companies will enter and prices will tend to fall. Companies will have to operate on shrinking profit margins towards the end of the 90s. Close to the year 2000 the market will have reached maturity as the mar-

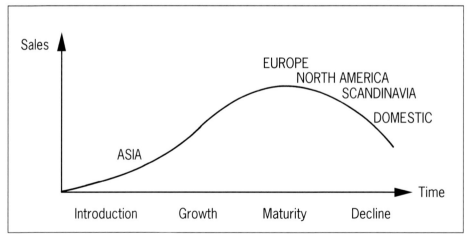

Figure 3.6.1. *The market research results for Master in the various markets.*

ket stabilizes or even declines in size."

The illustration in figure 3.6.3 is included in the consultant's report.

In late December 1985 Beta presents its new strategy:

Mission: To meet demanding customers future needs.

Objective: To become the market leader in North America and the world leader in research and development.

Strategy Plan: Master will be phased out. Avant will not be developed. Excel will have to be developed and sold until Optima is able to generate enough volume.

The new products will be made on lines. The old factory will be sold and newer buildings will be used instead. Advanced products have to be sold on advanced markets. North America is our main target market, but Europe will be phased in as Master is phased out.

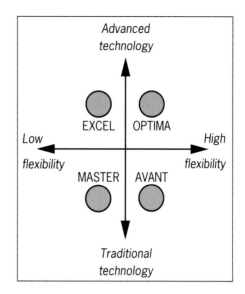

Figure 3.6.2. *The products can be placed in submarkets of their own on the basis of their flexibility and the technology used.*

We will need substantial support from our bankers in order to carry out investments and the marketing cam-

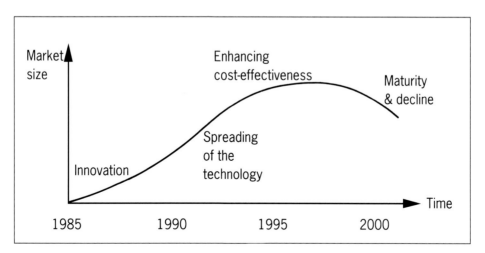

Figure 3.6.3. *The illustration in this figure is included in the consultant's report.*

paigns required to generate turnover. This strategy exploits our strengths and attempts to remedy our weaknesses. We feel compelled to develop both new markets and new products. We are aiming at intensive growth through diversification.

3.7 Case Study 2: How Beta is coping in 1991

Five years later we are again talking to Beta's managers about strategy, to find out how successful the strategy they developed in 1985 has been.

First we ask about the product portfolio. Beta's managers explain:

"None of our products has developed into a star - yet. We now realize that further investments will be required if Excel and/or Optima are to become stars. Master has remained a cash cow without which our investment program would have failed. Now Excel is developing well and the time might be ripe to phase out Master."

Beta's management team is aware of the relative crudeness of the Boston Consulting Group's model. A conside-rable amount of time and effort is also being spent to analyze the products according to General Electric's strategic business planning grid. Their findings are shown in figure 3.7.2.

In their evaluation of the industry the managers take several factors into account: size, growth potential, price, competition, trade barriers, etc. The company's business strength is evaluated primarily on the basis of size, growth, market share, profitability and image.

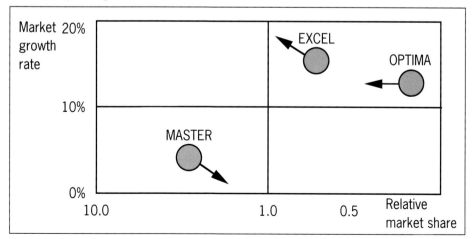

Figure 3.7.1. *Using the Boston Consulting Group's growth-share matrix, Beta's product portfolio can be illustrated as shown above.*

115

Master has low industry attractiveness because of decining prices, slow growth and stiff competition. Excel and Optima both look good in terms of growth and price trends.

Master has high business strength mainly because of market share. Beta's market position with regard to Excel and Optima is still unclear, so these products have medium strength.

Continuing with the General Electric model, Beta analyzes its market portfolio. Market attractiveness depends on size, growth, the legal system, and economic stability. Business strength

relative to the market focuses on adaptation to local needs, quality of the sales organization and after-sales service. The results are shown in figure 3.7.3.

The domestic market provides a safe home base, but without any additional potential. Efforts in Europe have turned out to be quite successful. Beta has not yet achieved its strategic objective of becoming the market leader in North America. More investment will be needed to reach that goal.

The results are encouraging, and Beta's management team plans to stick to its strategy. The members viewed the

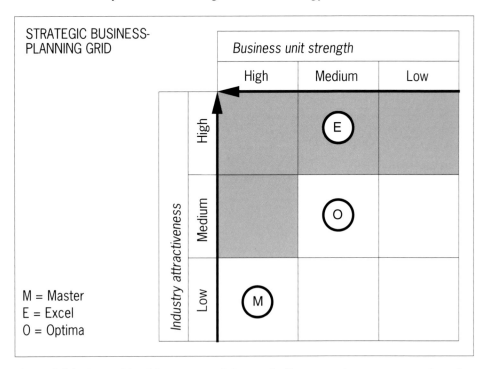

Figure 3.7.2. *A considerable amount of time and effort was also spent to analyze the products according to General Electric's strategic business planning grid. The findings are shown above.*

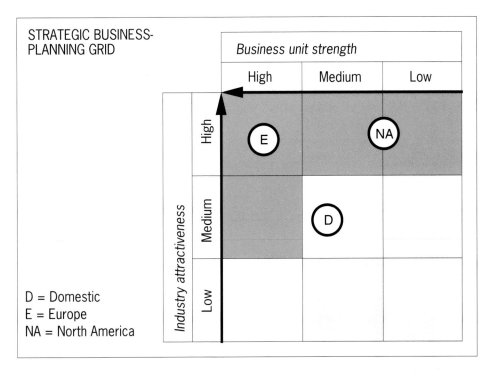

Figure 3.7.3. *Business strength relative to the market focuses on adaptation to local needs, quality of the sales organization and after-sales service.*

analyses of the situation in 1991 as support for the strategy they have chosen. But certain objectives have still not been achieved. The management is concerned about getting stuck in the middle, as Michael Porter puts it. A company that fails to develop and exploit an advantage over its competitors will get stuck in the middle of Porter's U-curve (see figure 3.7.4 on the next page).

We see from the graph in figure 3.7.4 that a company can succeed by being big and profitable, or by being small and profitable. We thus identify two generic strategies: Cost superiority and focusing (see figure 3.7.5 on the next page). If you can produce at relatively low cost, go for high volume and large market share. If not, you have to focus on products that a smaller company can develop the special skills to produce. Not daring to be different and trying to do everything will put you in the middle...

... and that is not the place to stay in!

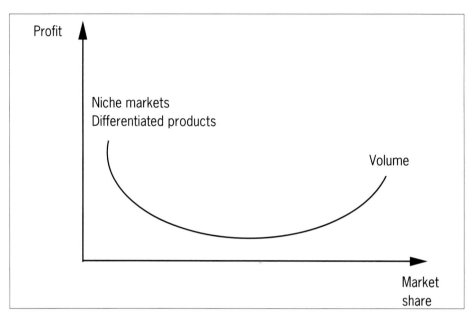

Figure 3.7.4. *A company that fails to develop and exploit an advantage over its competitors will get stuck in the middle of Porter's U-curve.*

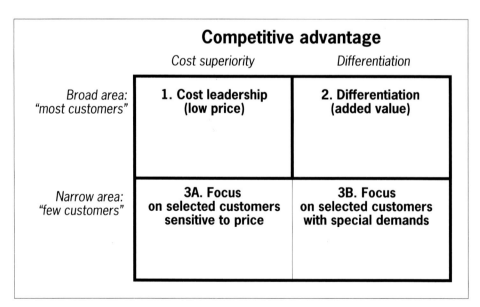

Figure 3.7.5. *Porter's primary postulate is simple: "If you cannot be best where you are, then move!"*

Sources and suggested readings

(1) Ansoff, I. "Strategies for Diversification," *Harvard Business Review*, Sept-Oct 1957, pp 113-124

(2) Copeland, E. and Weston, J.F., *Financial Theory and Corporate Policy*, third edition, Addison-Wesley, 1988.

(3) *The Economist*, various issues.

(4) Kotler, P., *Principles of Marketing*, Prentice-Hall, 1980.

(5) Stoner, J., *Management*, second edition, Prentice-Hall, 1982.

(6) Porter, M., *Competitive Strategy*, The Free Press, 1980.